God's First Letter
To Timothy

Roger Henri Trepanier

© 2021

This book is dedicated to the memory of Harold Fiss; elder, mentor, and friend, who has now departed to be with our Lord and Savior, Jesus Christ!

Titles available from Roger Henri Trepanier in The Truth Seeker's Library™ series:

God Did Not Create Human Beings To Die… But To Live On…
Eternally!
Finding Comfort And Encouragement In The Promises Of God In The
Last Days
How We Know For Sure That We Are Living In The Last Days!
Have You Ever Wondered What Happens After Death?
An Introduction To The New World That Is Coming On The Earth
Deeper Truths Of The Christian Life
Evangelism As God Intended
Keeping On Serving God In The Last Days
The Mysterious World Of Angels And Demons
No One Loves As He Loves!
Thanks Be To God For His Indescribable Gift!
The Church Is Very Much Alive, Well, And Growing!
Tracing The Steps Of The Son Of God From Eternity To Eternity!
War, And Going To War, Is Simply Not Of God!
God Never Meant Prayer To Be A Mystery!
Health Is One Of God's Great Blessings!
Removing The Mystery Surrounding Baptism!
This World's Return To Paganism Is Almost Complete!
Removing The Mystery Surrounding Heaven!
God's Covenants Were Meant For Mankind's Blessing!
The Four Ages Of Time
The Awesomeness Of God!
A Call To A Biblical Christianity!
Believers! Look Up! Our Homegoing Is Any Day!

**Titles available from Roger Henri Trepanier in The Practical
Helps Library™ series:**

Learning to Overcome The Perplexities Of This Present Life
So, I Hear You Want To Work With Seniors?
I Will Not Have This Man To Rule Over Me!
Spiritual Truth To Warm The Heart!
Fasten Your Seatbelts: Turbulence Ahead!
Living A Normal Christian Life In An Increasingly Abnormal World!
If You Have Jesus; You Do Not Need Drugs!
To Do God's Will Is To Have A Foretaste Of Heaven!

This World Is Ready For The Rule Of The Antichrist!
President Trump And The Q Movement Versus Satan And The Deep State
More Of God's Great Promises For Comfort And Encouragement!
Alert! The C-Virus Pandemic Was Satan's Practice Run For A New World Order
The Days Are Evil! The Time Is Short! Be Saved From This Perverse Generation!
Your Worldview Determines Your Wellbeing And Eternal Destiny!
What We Are Watching Is The Spirit Of The Antichrist At Work!

Titles available from Roger Henri Trepanier in The Christian Fiction Library™ series:

The Beginning Of A New Dawn
It Is Never Too Late For Love!
The True To Life Musings Of Fred And Ernie
Between A Rock And A Hard Place!
Love Knows No Boundaries!
A Woman Worth Pursuing!
Love Is More Than Just A Four Letter Word!
The Twists And Turns Of The Life Of Faith!

Titles available from Roger Henri Trepanier in The Word Of God Library™ series:

God's First Letter To The Thessalonians
God's Second Letter To The Thessalonians
God's Letter To Believers Through Jude
God's Three Short Letters To Believers Through John
God's Letter To Scattered Believers Through James
God's Letter To Titus
God's Prophetic Word To Mankind Through Daniel
God's Letter To Philemon And God's Letter To The Colossians
God's Consummation Of All In The Book Of Revelation
God's Letter To The Philippians
God's First Letter Through Peter
God's Second Letter Through Peter
Jonah, God's Reluctant Prophet!
God's Letter To The Galatians
God's Providence In The Book Of Esther

God's Love For Gentiles In The Book Of Ruth
God's Letter To The Ephesians

God's Love For Gentiles In The Book Of Ruth
God's Letter To The Ephesians

INTRODUCTION

This is the eighteenth book in the series titled, "The Word of God Library." God is leading His servant to have a few commentaries published which are the result of over 40 years of study, combined with practical experience. And while these commentaries are expository in nature (that is, explained in some detail), they are still intended to be devotional, heartwarming, and as practical as possible to help believers live out their faith in these last days of the present third age of time.

And there are four things that we should be aware of at the outset. The first is that the Biblical text that God gave, and which makes up God's First Letter To Timothy, will be included as part of the text of this book, so that the reader will not have to turn to the Bible to read that text. It will appear in italics. Then secondly, each chapter has been broken into smaller sections, which will begin with italicized text, with a brief explanation supplied as a help of what is covered in that particular section. And thirdly, whenever an added word appears in the Biblical text that was supplied by the translators from the original Greek into English as a help to the reader, it will be noted. Then fourthly, at times comments are supplied by the author, which will be in brackets in the text of God's word as an additional help to the reader.

Then we are to also note that there is an Addenda at the back of the book with four sections. In Addendum A, there is a brief outline of the four ages of time, for any reading the book who might not be familiar with this information. Then in Addendum B, there is a brief outline of the two comings from Heaven to earth in time of God's Son, The Lord Jesus Christ, for any who may not be familiar with this information either. In Addendum C, we have we have a presentation of what the relation is in a local church between elders and those ministers referred to as apostles, prophets, evangelists, and shepherd/teachers. In Addendum D, we have a presentation of the gospel, which is the good news that God gives in His word regarding His Son, The Lord Jesus Christ, for any readers who might not have as yet this vital personal relationship with God, through faith in His Son.

What should also be mentioned before closing this Introduction, because we are all somewhat curious by nature, is that after completing 21 years of formal education and then spending almost 28 years working in Project Engineering and Management in the Corporate offices of two large utilities, God called His servant as a non-denominational evangelist in early 1999, and then sent him out over two thousand miles, away from family and friends, to the place of service God assigned, which is where His servant has been and is still serving Him as evangelist, author, and counselor. The author is a widower with three adopted children, all now married with a family of their own.

Please note the two websites listed below, which have been established for the purpose of interacting with readers and for gospel ministry:

http://www.pilgrimpathwaypublications.com

http://servantofmosthigh.com

And now my prayer is that God will richly bless you as you read this book, and greatly minister to your every need in your life, as only God can! To Him be all praise, honor, and glory, with thanksgiving, both now and forevermore! Amen.

CONTENTS

CHAPTER ONE

1 Timothy 1:1-20

1 Timothy 1:1, God identifies the human vessel through whom He gave us this letter

As we begin God's first letter to Timothy, we note from 1 Timothy 1:1 that God there lets us know the human vessel through whom He gave us this letter, *"Paul, an apostle of Christ Jesus according to the commandment of God our Savior, and of Christ Jesus, who is our hope…"* As we see here, Paul was the human vessel whom God chose to give us this letter through, whom we then see identifies himself as "an apostle of Christ Jesus…"

We need to note that in saying this, the apostle Paul does not here refer to himself as one of the twelve original apostles, which God's Son personally chose while here on earth at His first coming from Heaven, as we see for instance at Luke 6:13. But rather, he is referring to himself as one of the apostles that God raised up AFTER His Son had returned to Heaven again in the ascension. For while God's Son was on earth, Paul was still Saul the unbeliever, who did not come to personally know God in salvation until after God's Son appeared to him from Heaven, as we see at Acts 9.

The word "apostle" here means 'one sent out,' which in the case of Paul was something that occurred at Acts 13:1-4, which was also when Barnabas was sent out by God. We then note that shortly after this, as we see at Acts 14:14, both Paul and Barnabas were now being referred to by God as "apostles." Both were now apostles "of Christ Jesus," due to the fact that He was their Head in Heaven giving them directions from there, as also The Head of His whole body of believers on earth, as we see at Ephesians 1:22,23. For what needs to be grasped here and kept in mind is that as one is saved by God during the present third age of time, one is at that same moment indwelt of The Holy Spirit, Who not only cleanses of all sins ever committed against God and grants eternal life with God at that very moment of indwelling, but also unites one to God's Son in Heaven and to every other believer on earth, which together form the spiritual body of God's Son, known as the church of God during the present third age, noting 1 Corinthians 12:12,13,27.

Since all things originate with God The Father (noting 1 Corinthians 8:6), then "the commandment" for Paul to become an apostle came from God the Father, Whom we also see being referred to as "our Savior" here, since God The Father ever indwells, works through, and speaks through His Son by The Holy Spirit, noting for instance what God's Son told His disciples at John 14:10, while on earth at His first coming, "Do you not believe that I am in the Father, and the Father is in Me? The words that I say to you I do not speak on My own initiative, but the Father abiding in Me does His works," and also noting what God tells us at 2 Corinthians 5:18,19, "[18] Now all these things are from God (The Father), who reconciled us to Himself through Christ and gave us the ministry of reconciliation, [19] namely, that God (The Father) was in Christ reconciling the world to Himself, not counting their trespasses against them, and He has committed to us the word of reconciliation." The apostle Paul was led of God to add here, "and of Christ Jesus," as also being involved in his being an apostle, simply because it is through His Son that God The Father always works through.

We further note from verse 1:1 here that Paul refers to God's Son as "our hope," meaning that God's Son is the hope that all believers have by virtue of the fact that God's Son has been raised from the dead already and has now ascended back to Heaven and is at His Father's right Hand, which means that since we are united with Him through salvation, that this too is our hope one day, to be with Him in Heaven after our life here on earth in these present bodies is over. So the believers "hope" is to have life with God in Heaven past the grave, based on the work of God's Son on behalf of believers, in His death for sins, His burial, His resurrection from the dead, and His ascension to Heaven again. This is a hope that unbelievers do not have and never will have, noting 1 Thessalonians 4:13!

God is then seen to continue and now identifies the human vessel that the apostle Paul was now to write down this letter from God for, noting what we now read at 1 Timothy 1:2, *"To Timothy, my true child in the faith: Grace, mercy and peace from God the Father and Christ Jesus our Lord."* Here we see that this letter is being addressed to a believer named "Timothy," and since two letters will be seen as being sent to him by God, then that is why this letter is called "God's First Letter To Timothy."

So the first question we would have here is: Who is this Timothy? For we note that God does not send just one letter to him, but two letters were sent to him, which God does not do for any other believers in the course of all 66 letters He gave as part of His word, the Bible! First then, we note that the apostle Paul is led of God is refer to Timothy here as, "my true child in the faith…" The word "my" here is an added word by the translators of the original Greek text into English, which tells us that the translators believe that the apostle Paul was instrumental in having led Timothy to faith in God's Son for salvation, although the original here only lets us know that the apostle Paul, in personally knowing Timothy, believed him to be a true believer!

This then brings up the question here of whether the apostle indeed was the one who led Timothy to faith in The Lord Jesus Christ for salvation? If we turn to Acts 16:1-3 for a moment, which is when Timothy is not only mentioned for the first time in God's word, but this is also the occasion when the apostle Paul has his first contact with him, we will then have our answer. And so, we there read, "[1] Paul came also to Derbe and to Lystra. And A DISCIPLE WAS THERE, NAMED TIMOTHY, the son of a Jewish woman who was a believer, but his father was a Greek, and he was well spoken of by the brethren who were in Lystra and Iconium. [3] PAUL WANTED THIS MAN TO GO WITH HIM and circumcised him because of the Jews who were in those parts, for they all knew that his father was a Greek."

What is clear from these verses is that Timothy was already a believer when the apostle Paul first met him at Lystra, which was then a city in the province of Galatia, which was at the time part of the Roman Empire, which was ruling the known world. At the time that Timothy lived there, this whole area was known as Asia minor, but today forms part of the country we know as Turkey.

So coming back to verse 1:2, we see that the translators should NOT have added the word "my" here, but should just have rendered this as, "To Timothy, true child in the faith," for that was what Timothy indeed was when the apostle Paul first met him, namely a child of God and a disciple of The Lord Jesus Christ. Since we see from Acts 16:1 that Timothy's mother was a believer, this could have been how Timothy first came to personally know God in salvation, although we are later told by God at 2 Timothy 1:5 that his grandmother was also a believer, as we read there of what the apostle Paul says to Timothy in that verse, "For I am mindful of the sincere faith within you, which first dwelt in your grandmother Lois and your mother Eunice, and I am sure that it is in you as well."

We further see from Acts 16:2 that because Timothy was well spoken of by the other believers of the area, the apostle Paul wanted to take him along on his preaching of the gospel from place to place in the then known world. We also learn that Timothy's father was a Greek, while his mother was Jewish. And since the apostle Paul is said to have circumcised Timothy meant that Timothy's father was most likely an unbeliever.

We need to keep in mind here that under the new covenant – which we are now in during this third age of time, which started with the coming of The Holy Spirit to indwell believers, as we see at Acts 2:1-4 – circumcision of flesh was no longer a requirement of God, noting for instance what God tells us at Galatians 5:6, "For in Christ Jesus neither circumcision nor uncircumcision means anything, but faith working through love." However, since the apostle Paul's gospel ministry was to all nations (noting Acts 22:14,15), meant that he would be encountering unsaved Jews, and since the apostle Paul did all things for the sake of the gospel (noting 1 Corinthians 9:19-23) further meant that for this reason he circumcised Timothy before taking him along with him.

What we should also be aware of here is that out of all the traveling companions of the apostle Paul that we see mentioned in God's word, none is mentioned more often that Timothy, which as we will see as we continue through God's First and Second Letter To

Timothy, being one indication that it had been God, Who had been at work in the life of Paul to make him willing to bring Timothy along with him, and also to make Timothy willing to leave family and friends in order to travel the known world as a co-worker of the apostle Paul!

Another likely reason for the apostle Paul wanting to take Timothy along with him was not only that he was "well-spoken of by the brethren of Lystra and Iconium," as we have seen from Acts 16:2, but because of what the apostle Paul later disclosed of Timothy when he was led of God to write to the believers at Philippi what we read at Philippians 2:19-21, "[19] But I hope in the Lord Jesus to send Timothy to you shortly, so that I also may be encouraged when I learn of your condition. [20] For I have no one else of kindred spirit who will genuinely be concerned for your welfare. [21] For they all seek after their own interests, not those of Christ Jesus."

What also needs to be kept in mind as we continue is that whereas Paul was an apostle, nevertheless, Timothy will be seen as being referred to at 2 Timothy 4:5 later as being an evangelist. And in order to briefly explain the difference, we should note Ephesians 4:11 at this point, where we read, "And He (God's Son) gave some as apostles, and some as prophets, and some as evangelists, and some as pastors and teachers (this here being a dual gift in the one man, which should have been rendered as 'shepherd/teachers' by the translators, as the word 'pastor' is not a Biblical term. Wherever the Greek word in view here is used in Scripture, it is always rendered as 'shepherd' or 'shepherds').

What is important to grasp from this verse is that these men (and they are always males, never females in Scripture) were given by the ascended Son of God as gifts to His church on earth, so that apostles and prophets were for the foundation stage in the establishment of the early church (noting Ephesians 2:19-22), which lasted from approximately 33 AD, with the coming of The Holy Spirit to start the present third age, until approximately 90 AD, which was when God's book of Revelation was given to the apostle John for him to write down for us.

In other words, from the start of the present third age, God raised apostles and prophets in each of the local churches on earth UNTIL all the letters of the New Testament had been given, which was before the end of the first century AD. Then AFTER all the letters of the New Testament had been given by God, there were no apostles and prophets raised of God in any local church on earth, but only evangelists and shepherd/teachers! However, there was obviously a transition period when both apostles and evangelists were on the scene, as we see both working together in the gospel ministry team of the apostle Paul, with Timothy the evangelist. We also have another man, that being Philip, being mentioned as being an evangelist at Acts 21:8. It is widely believed that this first letter from God to Timothy was written down by the apostle Paul around 62 AD.

As we continue at 1 Timothy 1:2, we see that God leads the apostle Paul to give the usual greeting when addressing one another by letter, saying there to Timothy, "…grace, mercy and peace from God the Father and Christ Jesus our Lord." In other words, saying here, 'may God's unmerited favor rest upon you, who has been spared from what you deserve, that being death due to sin, in order to be given what you do not deserve, which is the forgiveness of sins and eternal life with God, in order that you might henceforth and forever enjoy peace with God and the peace of God, as now a child of His!

1 Timothy 1:3-7, God leads the apostle Paul to remind Timothy what he was instructed to do while at Ephesus, as what he was to watch out for

As God continues, He now has the apostle Paul remind Timothy, as we see from 1 Timothy 1:3-7, what he was to do while at Ephesus, and what he was to watch out for, *"[3] As I urged you upon my departure for Macedonia, remain on at Ephesus so that you may instruct certain men not to teach strange doctrines, [4] nor to pay attention to myths and endless genealogies, which give rise to mere speculation rather than furthering the administration of God which is by faith. [5] But the goal of our instruction is love from a pure heart and a good conscience and a sincere faith. [6] For some men, straying from these things, have turned aside to fruitless discussion, [7] wanting to be teachers of the Law, even though they do not understand either what they are saying or the matters about which they make confident assertions."*

When the apostle Paul says to Timothy here at verse 1:3, "As I urged you upon my departure for Macedonia…," we are to regard this as simply a reference to what he verbally instructed Timothy to do as he asked him to remain on at Ephesus, while he was on his way to

Macedonia. Then while the apostle Paul was at Macedonia – which today is northern Greece – he was led of God to write down this letter for Timothy, which he then sent to him while Timothy was still at Ephesus, with further instructions, as we now have here.

God's first instruction to Timothy through the apostle Paul, as we see from verse 1:3, was "to remain on at Ephesus..." What this means then is that both the apostle Paul and Timothy were at Ephesus when the apostle Paul left for Macedonia from there. If we look at the first time that the apostle Paul visited Ephesus, as we see at Acts 18:18-21, we there find out that this was only a very short visit, being accompanied at the time only with Aquila and his wife Priscilla. Then after a considerable length of time, the apostle did make a second return visit to Ephesus, as we then see at Acts 19:1, this time staying for two years, as we see from Acts 19:10.

Then when the apostle Paul did leave Ephesus after that two-year stay, as we see from Acts 20:1, it was indeed to Macedonia that he next went to from there. Since the apostle Paul never made a return trip to Ephesus after this, then Timothy must have been with him during those two years that he was at Ephesus, and when he left to go to Macedonia, it was then that Timothy was told to remain there and given these further instructions.

Then God's second instruction to Timothy through the apostle Paul is at verse 1:3 and was to "instruct certain men not to teach strange doctrines;" which simply meant that there were unbelievers there at Ephesus, who were teaching things that was contrary to the faith, that is, that was contrary to what was contained in the word of God, and which the believers had believed as part of the faith they now held. The word "instruct" as used here in relation to these unbelievers does not adequately catch the thought, and should have been rendered as "command," "order," or "charge" instead. If these unbelievers were allowed to continue uninterrupted, then they would likely eventually lead some of the believers astray with these false teachings. So God obviously wanted this stopped, which Timothy was to do.

The third instruction that God led the apostle Paul to give to Timothy here is at verse 1:4, where we see that he was not to "pay attention to myths and endless genealogies..." In other words, he was to be careful not to get caught up in fables and fairy tales, which were the product of one's fertile imagination; nor was he to get caught up in tracing family histories, which could go on and on down every rabbit trail. We need to keep in mind that there were no computers in those days, where a lot of records are now kept, readily accessible, and easily checked.

It is obvious here that God did not want Timothy to be led astray from the truth of the faith, as these things would tend to occupy his mind if he were to allow himself to be led into them, with the end result being to give rise to further questions that would tend to lead into fanciful thoughts, "rather than furthering the administration of God which is by faith." In other words, God wanted Timothy to fulfill his responsibilities as part of the call of God on his life, which he could only do if he were to walk by faith, that is, to continue to trust God in everything, by looking to Him alone to guide, to provide, and to do all in him and through him by His grace and power!

God's end goal, that He wanted to see achieved through Timothy's instruction of others here, as we see at verse 1:5, was threefold: To have believers 1) love God and others from a pure heart; 2) walk before God and a watching world with a good conscience; and therefore 3) end up living a sincere faith, as one that would end up counting for both time and eternity!

As God goes on to point out at verses 1:6,7, there were others at Ephesus, in addition to those mentioned at verses 1:3,4 already, who were living in contrast to what God wanted to see from those who were believers, who were caught up in discussions that did not go anywhere and did not achieve anything in their having assumed themselves to be "teachers of the law" – which therefore meant here that these men were Jews, since the "law" in view here related to the first five books of the Old Testament, as given to mankind by God through Moses – "even though they do not understand either what they are saying or the matters about which they make confident assertions." In other words, these men were unbelievers and as such would not have The Spirit of God in them in order to properly discern the truth of God contained in the Scriptures they were trying to understand for themselves and teach others. Timothy, as God's servant there needed to be on the lookout for such people.

God then takes a moment to explain through the apostle Paul that His Law is indeed good, which He gave only for purposes that are in line with His will, as we now see at 1 Timothy 1:8-11, *"[8] But we know that the Law is good, if one uses it lawfully, [9] realizing the fact that law is not made for a righteous person, but for those who are lawless and rebellious, for the ungodly and sinners, for the unholy and profane, for those who kill their fathers or mothers, for murderers [10] and immoral men and homosexuals and kidnappers and liars and perjurers, and whatever else is contrary to sound teaching, [11] according to the glorious gospel of the blessed God, with which I have been entrusted."*

At verse 1:8 here, God points out that His Law in indeed good, when used as God intended it to be used when He gave it to mankind, not simply because God is the Lawgiver and has the right to make the laws for His creation, but also keeping in mind that all that comes from Him is always good! However, one has to also keep in mind, as God goes on to point out at verses 1:9,10, that His Law, contained in the first five books of the Old Testament, which was then condensed into His Ten Commandments, as we see at Exodus 20:3-17, was given to regulate the lives of mankind on earth, which means that those who are righteous – as those who live by God's righteous life which continues being imparted to those who live with no known unconfessed sins from the moment of one's salvation onward – do not need to be concerned about God's Law, since all God's Law is automatically being obeyed by God's power and grace as one lives by God's imparted life!

This further means then that God's Law applies only to those, who being yet unbelievers, are Law-breakers, namely "those who are lawless and rebellious, for the ungodly and sinners, for the unholy and profane, for those who kill their fathers or mothers, for murderers and immoral men and homosexuals and kidnappers and liars and perjurers...," which is self-explanatory here. And so, in summary, God's Law applies to all those who live contrary to God's Law! For God's Law is the expression of God's will, as how man should walk with a Holy and Righteous God while on earth, so that those who do not walk in accordance with His Law are not only Law-breakers, but make themselves enemies of God, subject to His judgment leading to death!

We note that at verses 1:10,11, God equates "sound teaching" with "the glorious gospel of the blessed God." In other words, in God's word, starting with His Law, as what is contained in the first five books of the Bible, namely Genesis, Exodus, Leviticus, Deuteronomy, and Numbers, God has made known, starting in the Old Testament, all that mankind needed to hear and believe, which centered on His Son, The Lord Jesus Christ, for one to enter into all the blessings of knowing and walking with God, and then eventually enter glory, which is Heaven, as Gods own abode!

For what also needs to be grasped here is that starting at Genesis 3:15 and onward, God speaks of His Son coming to earth one day in the future, as born of a woman, Who will, when He comes, undo all the works of the devil, which are sin and death, with this gospel truth being foreshadowed in God's word, until He came, through the animal sacrifices and offerings that God gave the nation of Israel to observe, as representative of all the nations of the earth! After God's Son had come to earth, that gospel truth was first made known in the first four books of the New Testament, that being, Matthew, Mark, Luke, and John, which was then expounded upon in the letters from God in the rest of the New Testament.

There are four truths in particular that we ever need to keep in mind whenever we encounter God making reference to the gospel. The first is that the word "gospel" means 'good news.' Secondly, the word "gospel" is God's good news relating always to His Son, The Lord Jesus Christ, noting Romans 1:1-4,9. Thirdly, the "gospel" relates specifically to what God's Son has done on behalf of a sinful human race in paying the penalty of death at the cross, in His burial to put those sins away, and His resurrection from the dead the third day, so as to be alive forevermore, for it is through God's that He imparts eternal life to those who come to believe in Him. Fourthly then, the gospel is God's only message that He has given that guilty sinners must believe for the forgiveness of sins and eternal life with God, noting Romans 1;16; 1 Corinthians 15:1-4; and Ephesians 1:13. God refers to His gospel at 1 Timothy 1:11 as His "glorious gospel," because it comes from glory, that is, from Him in Heaven, and leads one to glory, that is, to Him in Heaven!

God then leads the apostle Paul to add at the end of verse 1:11, in regards "to the glorious gospel of the blessed God," the words, "with which I have been entrusted," although in the apostle Paul's case, he was no longer entrusted with the good news relating to God's Son that foreshadowed Him as BEFORE He came to earth, namely in those animal sacrifices and offerings, bur rather now AFTER God's Son had come to earth with the body prepared for Him by His Father in the womb of that virgin woman (noting Hebrews 10:5), and now having already dealt with sin and death through His death at the cross, His burial, His resurrection from the dead the third day, and His subsequent ascension back to His Father's right Hand in Heaven!

1 Timothy 1:12-17, God leads the apostle Paul to expand on the truth that he was entrusted with, that being God's glorious gospel, by now giving a word of testimony to that effect

In having spoken of "the glorious gospel of the blessed God," with which the apostle Paul had been entrusted – and which was subsequently disclosed to mankind in the letters of the New Testament that God gave through him – God now leads him to expand on that truth and also add a word of testimony, as we now see at 1 Timothy 1:12-17, *"[12] I thank Christ Jesus our Lord, who has strengthened me, because He considered me faithful, putting me into service, [13] even though I was formerly a blasphemer and a persecutor and a violent aggressor. Yet I was shown mercy because I acted ignorantly in unbelief; [14] and the grace of our Lord was more than abundant, with the faith and love which are found in Christ Jesus. [15] It is a trustworthy statement, deserving full acceptance, that Christ Jesus came into the world to save sinners, among whom I am foremost of all. [16] Yet for this reason I found mercy, so that in me as the foremost, Jesus Christ might demonstrate His perfect patience as an example for those who would believe in Him for eternal life. [17] Now to the King eternal, immortal, invisible, the only God, be honor and glory forever and ever. Amen."*

At verse 1:12 here, we see the apostle Paul give thanks to God's Son, The Lord Jesus Christ, for having put Him in His service. And what we need to realize is that the apostle Paul is here making reference to the time when he was yet Saul, the unbeliever, whom God's Son then brought to faith in Himself, as we see the apostle

Paul give testimony to at Acts 9:1-19a; Acts 22:1-16; and Acts 26:1-18. Let us note from Acts 26:16-18 what God's Son said from Heaven to Paul, as yet Saul, when He first saved him, "[16] But get up and stand on your feet; for this purpose I have appeared to you, to appoint you a minister and a witness not only to the things which you have seen, but also to the things in which I will appear to you; [17] rescuing you from the Jewish people and from the Gentiles, to whom I am sending you, [18] to open their eyes so that they may turn from darkness to light and from the dominion of Satan to God, that they may receive forgiveness of sins and an inheritance among those who have been sanctified by faith in Me."

We also need to realize that here at verse 1:12, when the apostle is led to say, in relation to God's Son, "who has strengthened me, because he considered me faithful, putting me into service," that we should not think that he was put in service as an apostle due to any merit on his part, for all of salvation itself and afterwards is always, for any believer of any age of time, only a work of God's mercy, grace, working in and through one in the power of God and out of love! Let us notice what the apostle Paul was led of God to give testimony to at 1 Corinthians 15:10, which is true not only for the apostle Paul, but also for every believer in every age of time, "But by the grace of God I am what I am, and His grace toward me did not prove vain; but I labored even more than all of them, yet not I, but the grace of God with me."

Therefore, the reality to be grasped here is that in saving Saul the unbeliever, who then became Paul the believer, God's imparted life to him came with God's enablement to do all of God's will as part of the plan of God for his life. And once appointed to God's service, he was then found trustworthy and reliable only because of God's power at work in him! Let us note three verses that the apostle Paul himself gave in testimony in this regard, the one being what we read at Philippians 2:13, "for it is God who is at work in you, both to will and to work for His good pleasure;" a second is at Philippians 4:13, "I can do all things through Him who strengthens me," and the third is at Colossians 1:29, "For this purpose also I labor, striving according to His power, which mightily works within me."

Up to the point of God's Son saving his soul, the apostle Paul, as yet Saul, was, as he goes on to testify at verse 1:13, "formerly a blasphemer and a persecutor and a violent aggressor," since he was at that time intent on stamping out the faith in Christ Jesus that was just starting to spread outward from Jerusalem through the Twelve apostles (minus Judas Iscariot, and later adding Matthias, noting Acts 1:15-26) that God's Son had called to Himself, trained, and then sent out to carry on the ministry, after He had returned to Heaven in the ascension.

We see this in what God mentions of him at Acts 8:3 for instance, "But Saul began ravaging the church, entering house after house, and dragging off men and women, he would put them in prison," with the apostle Paul himself also giving testimony to this after God had saved him, as we see for instance at Acts 22:4, "I persecuted this Way to the death, binding and putting both men and women into prisons," and also at Acts 26:10,11, "[10] And this is just what I did in Jerusalem; not only did I lock up many of the saints in prisons, having received authority from the chief priests, but also when they were being put to death I cast my vote against them. [11] And as I punished them often in all the synagogues, I tried to force them to blaspheme; and being furiously enraged at them, I kept pursuing them even to foreign cities."

When the apostle Paul goes on at verse 1:13 and says, "I was shown mercy because I acted ignorantly in unbelief," he is here making reference to when God's Son saved his soul from the penalty of death, which he deserved, since mercy refers to God withholding from one the judgment that one rightly deserves. And so, instead of receiving the penalty of death at God's Hand that he deserved, the apostle Paul was instead given, as he goes on to say at verse 1:14, "the grace of our Lord was more than abundant, with the faith and love which are found in Christ Jesus."

God's grace here is a reference to His unmerited favor, as what the apostle Paul received at God's Hand, along with the faith to believe in God's Son, which brought him the forgiveness of sins and eternal life with God. And so, in coming to personally know God through faith in His Son, he was bestowed The Holy Spirit, Who in coming to indwell his human spirit at the point of believing, also filled him with the love of God, with both that faith and that love coming to him from God The Father through His Son by The Holy Spirit!

At verse 1:15, the apostle Paul continues his word of testimony by saying that he has found the statement, "that Christ Jesus came into the world to save sinners," to be one that can be fully accepted, believed, and trusted in, because he, as one of the worst of sinners, had indeed now found this to be true in his own life, since God had saved him, one who did not deserve salvation! The apostle Paul no doubt would still remember to his dying day what he was and did as yet an unbeliever, noting for instance what we read at 1 Corinthians 15:9, "For I am the least of the apostles, and not fit to be called an apostle, because I persecuted the church of God."

Then at verse 1:16, the apostle Paul is led of God to make a very interesting statement – which I have found to be true in my own life as an evangelist and that of many other ministers as well – when he says, "Yet for this reason I found mercy, so that in me as the foremost, Jesus Christ might demonstrate His perfect patience as an example for those who would believe in Him for eternal life." In other words, in God selecting one of the worst sinners out there for Him to not only save, but to even render one of His ministers in His service, God is not only showing the extent of His mercy, but also showing to those who are not yet saved just how much patience He has in waiting for them to come to faith in Him and receive His eternal life!

What is not stated here, but which is also true from this, is that ministers who have experienced this great mercy from God are more likely to have empathy for every sinner that God does bring to eternal life in Himself. I have often expressed it this way: God often makes a minister by scraping the bottom of the barrel, so that one can then empathize with any sinner in the course of one's ministry that God saves further up in the barrel. For if one is the foremost of sinners, then how can one look down on a sinner that is not the foremost? And if one has experienced so great a mercy from God, then how can one not extend the same in kind to others?

And so, in having considered the extent of God's love, mercy, and grace in having saved his soul, despite his being one of the worst of sinners, the apostle cannot refrain from uttering a word of praise to God The Father in closing this brief word of testimony, by saying here at verse 1:17, "Now to the King eternal, immortal, invisible, the only God, be honor and glory forever and ever. Amen."

In the process of his being led to state this, we learn five great truths of the faith here. The first is that God is enthroned in Heaven as "King" over all His creation, which is true for both time and eternity, noting for instance what we read of Him at Revelation 15:3, "And they sang the song of Moses, the bond-servant of God, and the song of the Lamb, saying, "Great and marvelous are Your works, O Lord God, the Almighty; Righteous and true are Your ways, King of the nations!"

Then secondly, we also see the truth that God is indeed eternal, having no beginning or end. When the original creation took place, which was when time started to be marked (noting Genesis 1:14), God was already in existence as Father, Son, and Holy Spirit. The word rendered "eternal" here is "Aion" in the original Greek and refers to a period having an undetermined duration. We see God designated as "King eternal" here, which is as Supreme Ruler over all, for both time and eternity, both past and present.

Thirdly, we have the truth here that God is immortal, which word refers to the fact that God is not subject to decay, and therefore not subject to death. Human beings have a human body which is subject to decay, and therefore death, which is due to sin (noting Romans 5:12). Since God is forever sinless and does not have a perishable body, He is therefore immortal. That is why we are told later at 1 Timothy 6:16, "who alone possesses immortality."

Then fourthly, we have the truth here that God is "invisible," which means that He cannot ever be seen by any human being, either in the past, now, or in the future; not even in eternity to come. That is why God gave His Son, The Lord Jesus Christ, Who is, for both time and eternity future, the visible expression of God The Father (2 Corinthians 4:4; Colossians 1:15; Hebrews 1:3). In seeing God's Son, one sees God The Father (noting John 14:9). Only God's Son and the unfallen angels have ever seen God The Father (noting John 1:18).

And lastly, we see the truth here at 1 Timothy 1:17 that God is "the only God." Even though God has made Himself known as Father, Son, and Holy Spirit during time (noting Matthew 28:19), nevertheless this is a disclosure of there being three distinct, Divine, and indivisible Persons in only One God (noting John 5:44; 1 Corinthians 8: 6; Jude 1:25). Therefore, because all of this is true of our One God, then indeed to Him "be honor and glory forever and ever. Amen."

1 Timothy 1:18-20, God's command to Timothy, in light of the prophecies previously made concerning him

As God continues, He now gives Timothy a command through the apostle Paul, in light of prophecies previously made concerning him, as we now see from 1 Timothy 1:18-20, *"[18] This command I entrust to you, Timothy, my son, in accordance with the prophecies previously made concerning you, that by them you fight the good fight, [19] keeping faith and a good conscience, which some have rejected and suffered shipwreck in regard to their faith. [20] Among these are Hymenaeus and Alexander, whom I have handed over to Satan, so that they will be taught not to blaspheme."*

God's command to Timothy here consists of three parts, which are: 1) for him to "fight the good fight;" 2) for him to keep "the faith;" and 3) for him to maintain "a good conscience" in his walk with God. which he would be doing by continuing on in God's will each day, which would be achieved by his living by God's imparted life with no known unconfessed sins in His life. And God bases this command here "in accordance with the prophecies previously made concerning you," which brings up the obvious question of what these "prophecies" would be that are in view here?

The first thing we need to grasp is that these "prophecies" would have been uttered by New Testament prophets, as those, along with the apostles, who would have been raised of God during the foundation stage of God's church on earth, which was from the coming of The Holy Spirit, as we see at Acts 2:1-4, and until the full canon making up the New Testament had been given by God. So during this period, which included the time of the apostle Paul and Timothy as here in view, these New Testament prophets would be giving forth direct revelation from God to believers, with God later having much of this revelation given as part of the letters in permanent form making up the New Testament. An example of such prophets would be as we see for instance in the local church at 1 Corinthians 14:29-33. As earlier mentioned when looking at 1 Timothy 1:2, the apostles and prophets were replaced, with God then raising evangelists and shepherd/teachers after the full canon of the

New Testament had been given by God, which had happened before the end of the first century AD.

Secondly, we are to note that God does NOT disclose what those prophecies were here! We cannot speculate where God is silent, but we can give an example of this from what we earlier quoted regarding the apostle Paul at Acts 26:16-18, quoting this again here for illustration purposes, "16] But get up and stand on your feet; for this purpose I have appeared to you, to appoint you a minister and a witness not only to the things which you have seen, but also to the things in which I will appear to you; [17] rescuing you from the Jewish people and from the Gentiles, to whom I am sending you, [18] to open their eyes so that they may turn from darkness to light and from the dominion of Satan to God, that they may receive forgiveness of sins and an inheritance among those who have been sanctified by faith in Me." The only difference is that at Acts 26, this was said prophetically to Paul by God's Son directly from Heaven, whereas in Timothy's case at verse 1:18 above, whatever prophecies are there in view were said by one or more New Testament prophets here on earth, with God's Son speaking at that time through those New Testament prophets to Timothy!

Then at the end of verse 1:19 and at verse 1:20, we have God naming two men, these being Hymenaeus and Alexander, who were professing to be believers, but in whose lives it simply was not true that they were fighting the good fight, keeping faith and a good conscience before God, and therefore are earmarked here by God as having gone astray from the faith. Since the apostle Paul could not see the heart of these men, to know if they were true believers or not, he is simply led to state here that "I have handed over to Satan," these men, "so that they will be taught not to blaspheme."

What is meant by this is explained for us in what the apostle Paul was led of God to say at 1 Corinthians 5:5, where we read, "I have decided to deliver such a one to Satan for the destruction of his flesh, so that his spirit may be saved in the day of the Lord Jesus." In other words, if one is a true believer, who is in the process of going astray, then in handing one over to Satan, that person will be sifted like wheat by the devil, in terms of experiencing many sorrowful things at the hands of the devil, so that if this person is really a true believer, then one will learn through these painful experiences that there nothing to be gained from uttering "blaspheme," that is, of speaking contemptuously of the things pertaining to God, and one will turn to God in repentance. If one does not repent before death comes (noting as further examples here 1 Corinthians 11:27-32), then that person will not be lost, if a true child of God, but will still be in Heaven after death. The reason for this is that salvation is a gift from God, same as a physical birth into this world, with neither one occurring apart from the grace and power of God, and once having occurred cannot be undone!

CHAPTER TWO

1 Timothy 2:1-15

1 Timothy 2:1-4, God begins his further instructions to Timothy through the apostle Paul by pointing out that the first order of business is prayer

As God continues His first letter to Timothy through the apostle Paul, He now gives His first further instruction, which relates to the matter of prayer, as we see at 1 Timothy 2:1-4, *"[1] First of all, then, I urge that entreaties and prayers, petitions and thanksgivings, be made on behalf of all men, [2] for kings and all who are in authority, so that we may lead a tranquil and quiet life in all godliness and dignity. [3] This is good and acceptable in the sight of God our Savior, [4] who desires all men to be saved and to come to the knowledge of the truth."*

There is a reason for God placing an emphasis on prayer at the start here, which we are to see from what we read at Acts 6:4, "But we will devote ourselves to prayer and to the ministry of the word." What has just been quoted was said by the Twelve apostles that God's Son had called to Himself, trained, and then sent out to carry on the ministry after God's Son had returned to Heaven again, after His suffering and death at the cross and His resurrection from the dead. What we read at Acts 6:4 here then is a declaration that God's ministers – that is, his apostles and prophets, before the full canon of Scripture was given, and His evangelists and shepherd/teachers, after the full canon of Scripture had been given – have two spiritual tools given by God for ministry, which God's Son Himself made full use of while on earth at His first coming, and that is, "prayer and the ministry of the word."

What God does here at verse 2:1 is not just mention prayer alone, which is conversing with God by the enablement of The Holy Spirit in the name of God's Son, our only access; but also mentions what is generally seen as part of prayer, such as "entreaties," which are the making of requests to God, in terms of expressing a need or making a supplication; also "petitions," which involves interceding with God on behalf of others; and of course, "thanksgivings," which is self-explanatory.

And so the thought here at verses 2:1,2 is: 'Whether you are conversing with God by means of strictly entreaties, or prayers, or petitions, or thanksgivings, do so on behalf of all men, not just for some, and especially for those who are over you in a position of authority, from the highest position in the land to the lowest, so that as believers we might be free to serve God in the godly way that we should as His children yet on earth, which is in a manner where we are at peace internally and also free from external threats, showing forth a dignity that arises from taking the moral high ground, which is then seen by all in one's reverent way of living!'

What has just been said by God at verses 2:1,2 is something that is "good and acceptable" in God's sight, as we then see at verses 2:3,4, for the simple reason that in this way we will be vessels on earth that God can use for His purpose, with the primary one being to see people saved, that is, will come to a knowledge of the truth relating to God's Son, so that they too will experience life with God that we enjoy through their also being forgiven their sins and being bestowed God's own righteous and eternal life to live by.

What needs to be kept in mind here is that when God first created mankind, He created us for Himself, that we, as a human race, might serve Him willingly, gladly, and unreservedly, out of love for Him! Of course, the entry of sin changed all that, but salvation can restore a human being to God's original intention for which one was created by God at the original creation!

We then see God continue and now reminds Timothy at 1 Timothy 2:5-6 that there is but one God and one Mediator between God and man, *"[5] For there is one God, and one mediator also between God and men, the man Christ Jesus, [6] who gave Himself as a ransom for all, the testimony given at the proper time."* At verse 1:4, God had there said that He desired all men to be saved and to come to a knowledge of the truth, with the key truth that one needs to know for that to occur being that there is only one way to God, which is through God's Son, Whom God The Father put forth to be The Mediator between a Holy God and a sinful human race!

When God's Son willingly left Heaven and took on the body that His Father had prepared for Him in the womb of the virgin (noting Hebrews 10:5), He, being then found in appearance on earth as a Man, He "gave Himself as a ransom for all," in that He humbled Himself and became obedient unto death, even death on a cross (noting Philippians 2:8), there paying the penalty of death due the sins of the human race. That is why God said at Acts 4:12, "And there is salvation in no one else; for there is no other name under heaven that has been given among men by which we must be saved," and also why God's Son could say at His first coming from Heaven to earth, what we read at John 14:6, "Jesus said to him, "I am the way, and the truth, and the life; no one comes to the Father but through (faith in) Me."

As we then see at 1 Timothy 2:7, God led the apostle Paul to give testimony to the fact that he was raised of God to share this truth with others, relating to the good news of God's Son, The Lord Jesus Christ, with the brackets here being part of the Biblical text, *"For this I was appointed a preacher and an apostle (I am telling the truth, I am not lying) as a teacher of the Gentiles in faith and truth."*

As we see here, the apostle Paul was led of God to share two specific truths that were true of him, the first being that God had appointed him "a preacher and an apostle." We have seen already that an "apostle" was 'one sent forth by God,' and now we further see that this sending forth by God was to be a "preacher," that is, God's messenger, who was to proclaim the gospel of salvation, which was

God's good news made known relating to His Son, namely that through faith in Him one could receive the forgiveness of sins and eternal life with God! The apostle Paul had earlier given testimony to this truth at 1 Timothy 1:11, when he had there been led of God to say, "according to the glorious gospel of the blessed God, with which I have been entrusted."

Then the second truth that the apostle Paul is here led of God to testify to is that he had also been appointed by God to be "a teacher of the Gentiles in faith and truth." In other words, it had been specifically to the Gentile nations of the world (which excluded Israel) that God had sent the apostle Paul to (noting Galatians 1:15,16), in order to preach the gospel of salvation, which related to the death of God's Son as payment for sins of the human race, His burial, and His resurrection from the dead the third day.

1 Timothy 2:8-15, instructions to Timothy on how believing males and believing females are to conduct themselves when gathered together for worship as a local church

We then see from 1 Timothy 2:8-15 that God now proceeds to give Timothy instructions regarding what believing males were to do and what believing females were to do and refrain from doing when gathered together for worship as a local church. Let us note to begin with what God's instruction is to believing males at 1 Timothy 2:8, *"Therefore I want the men in every place to pray, lifting up holy hands, without wrath and dissension."* As we see here, God wants Timothy to know (and us also) that it was the believing males, who were to pray audibly and publicly, as prompted and then led of The Holy Spirit. And let us also note here that this was to be done while "lifting up holy hands," and not holy arms, as is commonly seen so often, when supposedly viewing believers worshipping God, whether in person or on television, or on the internet.

When God says "holy hands" here, He is presuming that when one lifts one's hands to pray to God on behalf of the other believers gathered for worship that this is being done with a pure heart, that is, with no known unconfessed sins in one's life. The same is true here when God adds "without wrath or dissension." In other words, prayer is to be unto God from a pure heart, and especially public prayer, with one being at peace with all gathered, so that prayer is not being used as a way to point out the faults of any that might or might not be

34

present! God will never lead a believing man to pray publicly who has a grudge against anyone, or is not right with God!

Then at 1 Timothy 2:9-12, God gives Timothy instructions as to what believing females were to do and refrain from doing when gathered together with the believing males for the public worship of God as a local church, *"[9] Likewise, I want women to adorn themselves with proper clothing, modestly and discreetly, not with braided hair and gold or pearls or costly garments, [10] but rather by means of good works, as is proper for women making a claim to godliness. [11] A woman must quietly receive instruction with entire submissiveness. [12] But I do not allow a woman to teach or exercise authority over a man, but to remain quiet."*

God begins here by first pointing out at verses 2:9,10 what the PERSONAL APPEARANCE of the believing females is to be when gathering for the public worship of God as a local church, which is "to adorn themselves with proper clothing, modestly and discreetly, not with braided hair and gold or pearls or costly garments…" In other words, the believing females are not there to attract attention to themselves, in that they are not there to find a mate, nor are they there to parade how much jewellery they have or any of the costly outfits they might have; but rather they are there to focus on God for praise, thanksgiving, and adoration! In other words, God is looking for an outward appearance and inward condition of heart that is in line with one "making a claim to godliness," that is of being not only a believer, but one who walks in a Godly way, in that one is living by God's imparted life with no known unconfessed sins in one's life!

We also need to keep in mind that God is aware that the believers gathering together will be from various socio-economic groups, with some being poor, and some wealthy, with many in between. Therefore, the gathering of believers, especially in regards to the females, is that no females should feel out of place from being in the gathering based on outward appearances! What God is looking for is for all to be done so as to please Him, not for self-aggrandizement!

Then secondly, we see that at verse 2:11, God now addresses how the believing females are to BEHAVE while gathered for the public worship of God as a local church, in that "a woman must quietly receive instruction with entire submissiveness." In other words, the females are to be there as God commands at 1 Corinthians 14:34,35,

"The women are to keep silent in the churches; for they are not permitted to speak, but are to subject themselves, just as the Law (that is, God's word) also says. If they desire to learn anything, let them ask their own husbands at home; for it is improper for a woman to speak in church."

Since the above is God's command for females when gathered in the public worship as a local church, then the third instruction to them here, as given to Timothy, is as we see at verse 2:12, "But I do not allow a woman to teach or exercise authority over a man, but to remain quiet." What we are to grasp from this is that God NEVER raises, nor sanctions, a female to any ministerial position in the local church. In other words, no females, for instance, were chosen by God's Son as an apostle, even though there were many believing females that were part of His followers while He was on earth at His first coming from Heaven to earth. Nor do we see God gift any females as a prophet or an evangelist or as a shepherd/teacher in the local churches.

It is important to see that God in not being unfair toward the females here, but rather that He did establish SPECIFIC ROLES for males and for females in ALL SPHERES OF LIFE, whether that be in the home, in the workplace, the local church, or society in general. God touches on those roles for males and females when He goes on and says to Timothy, by way of the apostle Paul, what we now read at 1 Timothy 2:13-15, *"[13] For it was Adam who was first created, and then Eve. [14] And it was not Adam who was deceived, but the woman being deceived, fell into transgression. [15] But women will be preserved through the bearing of children if they continue in faith and love and sanctity with self-restraint."*

Here God is seen to give three reasons for the roles for males and for females that He wanted to see in the sphere of the local church gathering at verses 2:8-12 above. The first reason that God gives for these roles is that "it was Adam who was first created, and then Eve." In other words, the male and his role under God was His first priority when He set about to carry out the original creation at the beginning, as when time also began to be marked. God expands on this truth at 1 Corinthians 11:7-10, where He is there addressing the fact that men should not have their heads covered in the gathering of the local church, but the women should, giving here the reasons why, "[7] For a man ought not to have his head covered, since he is the image and glory of God; but the woman is the glory of man. [8] For man does not originate from woman, but woman from man; [9] for indeed man was not created for the woman's sake, but woman for the man's sake. [10] Therefore the woman ought to have a symbol of authority on her head (that is, a head covering), because of the angels."

However, even this might not suffice for some who are reading this, and so, what would prove useful here is noting what God says back at Genesis 2:18-24, which is at the beginning of when God was bringing His creation into being, "[18] Then the Lord God said, "It is not good for the man to be alone; I WILL MAKE A HELPER SUITABLE FOR HIM." [19] Out of the ground the Lord God formed every beast of the field and every bird of the sky, and brought them to the man to see what he would call them; and whatever the man called a living creature, that was its name. [20] The man gave names to all the cattle, and to the birds of the sky, and to every beast of the field, but for Adam there was not found a helper suitable for him. [21] So the Lord God caused a deep sleep to fall upon the man, and he slept; then HE TOOK ONE OF HIS RIBS and closed up the flesh at that place. [22] THE LORD FASHIONED INTO A WOMAN THE RIB WHICH HE HAD TAKEN FROM THE MAN, AND HE BROUGHT HER TO THE MAN. [23] The man said, "This is now bone of my bones, and flesh of my flesh; she shall be called Woman, because she was taken out of Man." [24] For this reason a man shall leave his father and his mother, and be joined to his wife; and they shall become one flesh."

And so, because the woman was fashioned out of man, that is why the man, Adam, could say at verse 23 above, "This is now bone of my bones, and flesh of my flesh…" And that is also why at verse 24, God says that when a man leaves home and finds a wife, they are no longer two people in God's sight, but "one flesh," in that now the woman is regarded by God as forming one unit, with God seeing the woman in the man. If there are children, then they too are seen as being part of the man. It is for this reason that throughout Scripture, God never numbers the females, nor the children, when viewing family units, since they are always viewed in the males. We see an example of this at Matthew 15:38 for instance.

What has just been said from Genesis above is also why God says to husbands and wives what we read at Ephesians 5:22-30, "[22] Wives, be subject to your own husbands, as to the Lord. [23] For the husband is the head of the wife, as Christ also is the head of the church, He Himself being the Savior of the body. [24] But as the church is subject to Christ, so also the wives ought to be to their husbands in everything. [25] Husbands, love your wives, just as Christ also loved the church and gave Himself up for her, [26] so that He might sanctify her, having cleansed her by the washing of water with the word, [27] that He might present to Himself the church in all her glory, having no spot or wrinkle or any such thing; but that she would be holy and blameless. [28] SO HUSBANDS OUGHT ALSO TO LOVE THEIR OWN WIVES AS THEIR OWN BODIES. HE WHO LOVES HIS WIFE LOVES HIMSELF; [29] FOR NO ONE EVER HATED HIS OWN FLESH, BUT NOURISHES AND CHERISHES IT, just as Christ also does the church, [30] because we are members of His body."

In the above passage, the reason that God calls the believing wives to be in voluntary submission to their husbands and calls the husbands to love their wives as Christ loves the church, as an indication of his submission to God's Son, is based on the principle that God gives at 1 Corinthians 11:3, "But I want you to understand that Christ is the head of every man, and the man is the head of a woman, and God is the head of Christ." In other words, God's Son voluntarily submitted to God His Father, when He humbled Himself to come to this earth to take on the body that His Father had prepared for Him in the womb of the virgin (noting Hebrews 10:5), for it was only in His doing so that He could through His voluntary submission to His Father provide for our redemption, as we read for instance at 1 Peter 3:18, "For Christ also died for sins once for all, the just for the unjust, SO THAT HE MIGHT BRING US TO GOD (through God then having a basis to forgive the sins and grant eternal life to all those who believe in Him for salvation), having been put to death in the flesh, but made alive in the spirit..."

And so, at Ephesians 5 above, the husband is called of God to voluntarily submit himself to His Head, Christ, by loving his wife as his own body; and the wife is in voluntary submission to God's Son when she voluntarily submits herself to her husband in everything. So coming back to 1 Timothy 2:13 above, the males and females are showing themselves to be in voluntary submission to God's Son in the sphere of the local church also, and not just the home, when they voluntarily submit themselves to God's commands to them in that sphere also!

Then coming to the second reason that God gives for the roles that He specifies for the females in the gathering of the local church, God is now seen to say at 1 Timothy 2:14, "And it was not Adam who was deceived, but the woman being deceived, fell into transgression." And what God has in view here is Genesis 3:1-6, which was after God had made Eve for Adam and they were now in the garden of Eden here on earth, which was a perfect, sinless environment, in that both Adam and Eve were still in innocence, not yet knowing good or evil, which meant they were as yet as sinless as when God first created them.

However, by this time (sometime after the end of Genesis 1 and before the start of Genesis 3), there had been an angelic being which had sinned against God in the realm of the heavens, who was then to become Satan, the devil. And at Genesis 3:1 here, we see Satan, in the guise of a serpent, come to Adam and Eve, and starts a conversation, which results in both Eve and Adam sinning against God, as the first sin to enter the human race here on earth, noting now what God tells us about this at Genesis 3:1-6, "[1] Now the serpent was more crafty than any beast of the field which the Lord God had made. And he said to the woman, "Indeed, has God said, 'You shall not eat from any tree of the garden'?" [2] The woman said to the serpent, "From the fruit of the trees of the garden we may eat; [3] but from the fruit of the tree which is in the middle of the garden, God has said, 'You shall not eat from it or touch it, or you will die.' " [4] The serpent said to the woman, "You surely will not die! [5] For God knows that in the day you eat from it your eyes will be opened, and you will be like God, knowing good and evil." [6] When the woman saw that the tree was good for food, and that it was a delight to the eyes, and that the tree was desirable to make one wise, she took from its fruit and ate; and she gave also to her husband with her, and he ate."

So what God means at 1 Timothy 2:14 when He says that it was not Adam who was deceived, but that it was Eve, He is there indicating that Adam's sin at Genesis 3:6, when he partook of the forbidden tree, was in direct disobedience to God's command to him at Genesis 2:16,17. However, in Eve's case, her sin was one of PRIDE, in that in God creating Adam, he was not only head of their home and the head over Eve, but he was also the chief spokesman for their family! What this meant here is that in Eve speaking out and answering the devil when he spoke to them, she was usurping the place that God had assigned to Adam. She was created by God as helpmeet to her husband, Adam, and not as the spokesmen for their family!

So when God says that Eve was deceived and fell into transgression, it was due to PRIDE, which was the very same sin by which that angelic being, who became Satan, the devil, sinned against God as the first sin to ever enter God's creation (noting Isaiah 14:12-14 and Ezekiel 28:12-15 in this regard). God also makes reference to Eve being deceived by the devil back at Genesis 3, when He says to the believers at Corinth through the apostle Paul at 2 Corinthians 11:3, "But I am afraid that, as the serpent deceived Eve by his craftiness, your minds will be led astray from the simplicity and purity of devotion to Christ." And so, this is the second reason that females were not given ministerial roles by God in the local churches, due to God knowing that the devil would have an easier time deceiving the females than the males.

And that then brings us to the third reason that God gives for the roles that He assigned to the males and females for all ages of time, being now seen from what He says at 1 Timothy 2:15, "But women will be preserved through the bearing of children if they continue in faith and love and sanctity with self-restraint." That is to say, women will be kept from the sin of pride "through the bearing of children," in that God has given them a very important role, which is to conceive and bear children into the world!

When looking at 1 Corinthians 11 above, we saw the importance of the man to God in what we quoted at verses 7 to 10. And now, we need to see from 1 Corinthians 11:11,12 the importance of the woman, not only to God, but to all mankind, "[11] However, in the Lord, neither is woman independent of man, nor is man independent of woman. [12] FOR AS THE WOMAN ORGINATES FROM THE MAN, SO ALSO THE MAN HAS HIS BIRTH THROUGH THE WOMAN; and all things originate from God." So what we are to grasp here is that to God, childbearing is a most important role, which has been assigned to the females only. So just as males do not seek this role assigned only to females by God, then too should the females restrain themselves from the roles assigned to the males by God!

So God concludes verse 2:15 by saying that the females will be kept from the sin of pride if they come to see the role of childbearing as God sees it and are satisfied with it as "they continue in faith and love and sanctity with self-restraint." The word "sanctity" here refers to one choosing a course of life that is fitting for one who has been set apart to serve God only; and the term "self-restraint" here refers to one needing to rein in desires and impulses that if given in to would lead one to be outside of God's will for one's life.

And so, the antidote to falling into the sin of pride for the females is to be satisfied in serving God in the role that He has assigned to them! Since God is not only our Creator, but also our Designer, He knew before the creation of human beings even took place what roles would satisfy each gender the most, and then created each gender with the makeup to best fulfill those roles! And surely we cannot fault God for what He has done and established for the sake of accomplishing His purposes during the ages of time, the foremost being the securing and effecting our redemption!

CHAPTER THREE

1 Timothy 3:1-16

1 Timothy 3:1-7, God specifying the qualifications for one to be appointed to the office of an overseer in a local church

After speaking of the roles of believing men and women in the local church at 1 Timothy 2:8-15, God now begins this third chapter in His first letter to Timothy by speaking, at 1 Timothy 3:1-7, of the spiritual qualifications that the men are to have, who are to be appointed to the oversight of a local church, *"[1] It is a trustworthy statement: if any man aspires to the office of overseer, it is a fine work he desires to do. [2] An overseer, then, must be above reproach, the husband of one wife, temperate, prudent, respectable, hospitable, able to teach, [3] not addicted to wine or pugnacious, but gentle, peaceable, free from the love of money. [4] He must be one who manages his own household well, keeping his children under control with all dignity [5] (but if a man does not know how to manage his own household, how will he take care of the church of God?), [6] and not a new convert, so that he will not become conceited and fall into the condemnation incurred by the devil. [7] And he must have a good reputation with those outside the church, so that he will not fall into reproach and the snare of the devil."*

When God starts out here and says, "This is a trustworthy statement," He is telling us that the instructions He is about to give us, relating to those having the oversight of a local church, is a word from God that can be relied upon in every case. In other words, a local church will be in line with God's will if it follows the instructions that God is about to give to Timothy for him to apply to the local church at Ephesus, where he presently was.

Then when God goes on here and starts speaking of "any man," this term is to be seen as being just one word in the Greek, which is a word that is always used in reference to males in God's word, never females. What this means then is that God definitely has a male in view here, relating to what He is about to give us instructions on!

So when God says, "if any man aspires," He is pointing out what a believing man would be seeking after, which we then see is "to the office of overseer…" What we are again to see here is that this term "office of overseer" in also one word in the original Greek, which simply means 'to the oversight.' In other words, for a man to aspire to the office of overseer in a local church simply means that one is seeking to be part of the oversight of that local church, for the oversight of any local church anywhere on earth is always a minimum of two men, as we will see shortly!

Since God then goes on and says of a man who seeks the oversight of a local church, "it is a fine work he desires to do," means that God is not putting any wet blankets on such desires, but rather encourages it. For whenever this happens, this means that God is at work in the life of such a believing man, for the "work" in view here is spiritual in nature, and like all Christian work, it is always carried out by the grace and power of God alone, or else it is not a work of God, but rather a 'work' that is of the flesh, having its origin in one's sinful nature, and would be sinful in God's sight.

What is important to grasp here is that whenever we see a man having the desire for such oversight, it is not only because it is God working in that man's life in order to bring him to the point of seeking that work, but also it would be God's desire and will in the first place to see that man actually being appointed to the oversight of a local church! Let us notice Acts 20:28 here as a further help in our understanding, "Be on guard for yourselves and for all the flock, among which THE HOLY SPIRIT HAS MADE YOU OVERSEERS (same word), to shepherd the church of God which He purchased with His own blood." Since a local church consists of believers, who are all children of God by a new spiritual birth into God's family that He alone brought about by His grace and power, then it only stands to reason that those who will have the oversight in a local church are going to be men that God Himself raises to that spiritual work!

God is very much aware of course that there will always be men who will seek such a work as either an occupation/career, or one doing so out of pride, in order to be over others, which would not be a true calling from God, as it should be in every case, if it is indeed God's work that is to be done in that local church. In that same passage at Acts 20, God goes on in the next two verses warning the leadership at the time that such an occurrence is always possible, as what was just mentioned above, noting here Acts 20:29,30 for our further instruction, "[29] I know that after my departure savage wolves will come in among you, not sparing the flock; [30] and from among your own selves men will arise, speaking perverse things, to draw away the disciples after them."

As God continues at verse 3:2, He now goes into the spiritual qualifications of a man having a God-given desire for the oversight of a local church, with God now saying, "An overseer, then, must be..." And before we get into what those spiritual qualifications are that those attending that local church will be able to observe in a man seeking such a work, is that God calls a man seeking the oversight of a local church "an overseer," which is an appropriate term that well suits the work, for it is the oversight that one would be providing, in terms of watching over the spiritual wellbeing of the flock of God on behalf of God!

But before we go too far here, there is something else we need to point out about that term "overseer," which is that elsewhere in God's word, God refers to such men as 'elders!' Let us note again Acts 20 here as an example. At verse 17 of Acts 20, we read, "From Miletus he (the apostle Paul) sent to Ephesus and called to him the ELDERS of the church," and then at verse 28, which was quoted above and which we will quote here again, we have these elders of verse 17 now referred to as "overseers," "Be on guard for yourselves and for all the flock, among which the Holy Spirit has made you OVERSEERS, to shepherd the church of God which He purchased with His own blood."

Before commenting further here, let us note another example, this time from what we read at Titus 1:5 to begin with, "For this reason I (the apostle Paul) left you in Crete, that you would set in order what remains and appoint ELDERS in every city as I directed you," and then noting verse 7, where God goes on to give somewhat similar spiritual qualifications as at 1 Timothy 3:2-7, noting Titus 1:7-9 here, "[7] For the OVERSEER must be above reproach as God's steward, not self-willed, not quick-tempered, not addicted to wine, not pugnacious, not fond of sordid gain, [8] but hospitable, loving what is good, sensible, just, devout, self-controlled, [9] holding fast the faithful word which is in accordance with the teaching, so that he will be able both to exhort in sound doctrine and to refute those who contradict." It is therefore clear, that whenever we see God speaking of an elder in the New Testament, He is speaking of a man having the oversight of a local church as an overseer!

But before we return to 1 Timothy 3:2 and look at what those spiritual qualifications are for an overseer, as an elder, there is something else which needs to be noticed, grasped, and remembered here. We earlier noted from Acts 16 that this was when Paul brought Timothy along with him, as part of his gospel ministry team. Then we noted that both Paul and Timothy spent two years ministering at Ephesus, Paul as an apostle and Timothy as an evangelist. Then at the end of that two-year period at Ephesus, the apostle Paul went to Macedonia and left Timothy at Ephesus. Then while at Macedonia, God gives this letter, which became First Timothy, for the apostle Paul to write down and send to Timothy, who was still at Ephesus. And as we just saw above, God now gives as part of that letter to Timothy the qualifications for an elder, as one who has the oversight of a local church as an overseer. What this means then is that there were no elders in that local church at Ephesus as yet. And what this further means is that as a result of God giving Timothy these spiritual qualifications through the apostle Paul, elders were then appointed by Timothy in the local church at Ephesus, which are then the elders that we see functioning as such at Acts 20:17, that we have also quoted!

And one obvious question here that might arise in the minds of some, is 'how' does one go about appointing elders, as no doubt Timothy did here in the local church at Ephesus, and which God directed the apostle Paul to lead Titus to do at Titus 1:5, that we have noted and note again here, "For this reason I left you in Crete, that you would set in order what remains and APPOINT ELDERS IN EVERY CITY as I directed you..." Before we answer the above question, we need to note that what we are looking at here was a God-ordained pattern that God wanted to see implemented, as new local churches were being established all over the known world, noting here what we see occurring earlier on in the apostle Paul's own gospel ministry, as we see at Acts 14:21-23, "[21] After they (that is, the apostle Paul and those in gospel ministry with him) had preached the gospel to that city and had made many disciples, they returned to Lystra and to Iconium and to Antioch, [22] strengthening the souls of the disciples, encouraging them to continue in the faith, and saying, "Through many tribulations we must enter the kingdom of God." [23] When they had APPOINTED ELDERS FOR THEM IN EVERY CHURCH, having prayed with fasting, they commended them to the Lord in whom they had believed."

And so, to answer the question posed above, elders were appointed in a local church by the apostle, or in Timothy's case, the evangelist, who had been the vessel of God by whom precious souls were saved in a locality, with those believers together forming the one local church of God. Then after a period of time, God The Father, through His Son at His right Hand by His Holy Spirit indwelling each of these believers of that local church would be at work in the lives of some of the believers, with God equipping those men in a spiritual way and then giving them the desire to be part of the oversight of that local church, which further meant that they would start functioning as such in an unofficial capacity.

Then the official appointment as elders would occur when the apostle, or in Timothy's case, the evangelist, would then recognize the men among the believers that God had already unofficially raised as elders (overseers) that He wanted to see be part of the oversight of that local church, noting here again for emphasis what God told the elders that we later see functioning there at Acts 20:28, "Be on guard for yourselves and for all the flock, among which THE HOLY SPIRIT HAS MADE YOU OVERSEERS, to shepherd the church of God which He purchased with His own blood."

The reader is encouraged to read Addendum C at this point, which is titled, "The relation of apostles and prophets, and of evangelists and shepherd/teachers to elders in a local church," before resuming the book at this point. The very important truth to see from Addendum C is that elders will be gifted men that God gives to each local church on earth, who would then function there as either an evangelist or a shepherd/teacher, as would be the case since the canon of Scripture has been given, which occurred before the end of the first century AD, which also means a minimum of two men for every local church that God does establish on earth.

As we now continue at 1 Timothy 3:2, we there see that God begins His spiritual qualifications of an elder, as one being part of the oversight of a local church as an overseer, as one who must be "above reproach," which term is again only one word in the original Greek, which refers to the fact that no one in the local church in which this man would already be unofficially functioning would be able to accuse or say anything against.

Then secondly, God says that an overseer must be… "the husband of one wife," which indicates at least six truths that we are to see here. The first is that an overseer should be a married man and not a single person. Secondly, this means that the overseer will be an older man, who has been married for a while, for at verse 3:4 God there talks of the overseer being the father of "children." And thirdly, in God saying "the husband," then God obviously has a male in view as an overseer. And fourthly, in God saying "of one wife," God obviously has a believer in view, since marriage between one man and one woman is an institution that God Himself established, as we see at Genesis 2:24, and which every believer will hold to and practice in one's life, so that one would not be cohabiting with a woman, which is not of God. A fifth truth for the mention of the "one wife" here would also speak of no divorce and no remarriage; for we are to see that since divorce is not of God (noting Matthew 19:3-6), then a divorced and remarried man would be regarded by God as having two wives!

Then a sixth truth to consider for the mention of a man being the husband of a "wife" would be due to the fact that elders will be exposed to many women during their ministry, both in their teaching, when the believers are gathered as a local church, and also when counseling. If one does not have a wife at home to meet one's needs as a man, then the devil will more easily have a field day with that man's thoughts when looking at those females. Let us notice here what God says at 1 Corinthians 7:1-5 in this regard, "[1] Now concerning the things about which you wrote, it is good for a man not to touch a woman. [2] But because of immoralities, each man is to have his own wife, and each woman is to have her own husband. [3]

The husband must fulfill his duty to his wife, and likewise also the wife to her husband. [4] The wife does not have authority over her own body, but the husband does; and likewise also the husband does not have authority over his own body, but the wife does. [5] Stop depriving one another, except by agreement for a time, so that you may devote yourselves to prayer, and come together again so that Satan will not tempt you because of your lack of self-control."

The third spiritual qualification that God says an overseer must have before being appointed by the evangelist to the oversight of a local church in an official capacity is "temperate," meaning 'even-tempered,' in terms of not blowing off the handle, not quick to overreact to comments or situations, so that one's temper remains under God's control at all times. Fourthly, "prudent," which speaks of a sound mind, where one's thoughts, desires, and impulses are under God's control. From what we are seeing here, it is obvious that the overseer must be one who is Godly, in terms of walking with God in one's daily life, so that one's thoughts, words, and actions will reflect that Godly life to others.

Then as a fifth spiritual qualification, God goes on to say at verse 3:2 that an overseer must be, "respectable," meaning living a well-ordered life, both inward and outward, which draws respect from others; then mentions a sixth spiritual qualification, which is, "hospitable," meaning one who loves and welcomes strangers, which refers to not just in one's home, but especially in the local church when gathered. We can be sure that the Diotrephes that God mentions at 3 John 1:9 was not an elder raised of God and was simply self-appointed!

Then a seventh spiritual qualification that an elder must have is to be, "able to teach." At Acts 6:4, God mentions there the only two tools, both spiritual, which all ministers raised of God have, which are "prayer and the ministry of the word." It does not matter if an elder has been gifted by God as an evangelist or a shepherd/teacher, all will have been enabled of God to teach His word to other believers, especially when gathered as a local church, if they have truly been raised of God to be an elder in the local church.

Then as an eighth spiritual qualification, God goes on to say that those appointed as elders must not be "addicted to wine," which term is also just one word in the original Greek, which means 'not given to wine.' The use of the word "addicted," inserted here by the translators from the Greek into English, is a poor translation, for the simple reason that on the surface it would appear that it is okay to drink wine as long as one is not addicted! But let us note what God led the apostle Paul to say to Timothy, as we will see later on in the book at 1 Timothy 5:23, "No longer drink water exclusively, but use a little wine for the sake of your stomach and your frequent ailments." As we see here, Timothy had understood the true meaning of what God had written to him earlier at verse 3:3, in terms of not being given to wine, which he was practicing in his own life. However, now the apostle Paul, under inspiration, advises him to take a little wine for medicinal purposes!

So what we need to grasp here is that even one drink of alcohol, whether that be liquor, beer, or wine, affects one's ability to control certain human functions in one's brain and physical makeup, so that one's senses are affected, so that in the state of drunkenness one is said to be impaired, in that one is no longer in full control of one's physiological functions!

We have likely all come across someone, who as a non-drinker, would act just like a person who was drunk, that is, intoxicated, with just one drink. I know, for my mother was such a person, and we used to laugh whenever she had a drink, for she would say or do outlandish things that she would never say or do under normal circumstances. And the reason we laughed is that we were yet children and yet unbelievers, not knowing about the import of this.

Because alcohol is intoxicating with even one drink, that is why God says to believers at Ephesians 5:18, "And do not get drunk with wine, for that is dissipation, but be filled with the Spirit." And so, God's will for those who are believers is to not to get drunk with wine, which starts with even one drink and is wasteful living, but instead believers should "be filled with the Spirit," where the word "filled" means to be under the control of The Holy Spirit! In other words, the starting point for believers knowing how to walk with God in a way that is not wasteful living, but instead is the wise way, where one makes the most of one's time while here on earth, is to be under the control of The Holy Spirit at all times, which God discloses as being His will for His own here!

And here is a truth worth keeping in mind in that regard, which is that when we are living by God's imparted life, which we are doing automatically when we are living with no known unconfessed sins in our lives, then WE ARE UNDER THE CONROL OF THE HOLY SPIRIT! And another truth that is closely related to this one which is worth remembering also is that when we are living by God's imparted life with no known unconfessed sins in our lives, we are 'living by faith,' which God also calls His own to do after salvation, noting Romans 1:17, Galatians 2:20; 3:11; and Hebrews 10:38!

And since God draws a contrast at Ephesians 5:18 between being under the control of wine – although He no doubt has all alcoholic and physiologically-altering substances in mind here – and between being under the control of The Holy Spirit – where He calls the former wasteful living and the latter part of His will for His own – we would be further instructed in this matter by noting what God tells us at Luke 1:13,15, "But the angel said to him, "Do not be afraid, Zacharias, for your petition has been heard, and your wife Elizabeth will bear you a son, and you will give him the name John… For he will be great in the sight of the Lord; and HE WILL DRINK NO WINE OR LIQUOR, AND HE WILL BE FILLED WITH THE HOLY SPIRIT WHILE YET IN HIS MOTHER'S WOMB."

God here has John the Baptist in view, whom God raised as a prophet to be the forerunner of His Son, The Lord Jesus Christ, to prepare people for His coming from Heaven to earth. And let us note here that in order to ensure that John the Baptist was always only under the control of The Holy Spirit, even from His mother's womb, and in order that John might only carry out God's will, he was not to ever partake of wine or liquor, which were both intoxicating. What God wanted people to know, once John the Baptist had started his public ministry, was that he was a servant of God, under God's control, here only to carry out God's will. Surely there is an important lesson there for all of us!

Then God goes on to a ninth spiritual qualification for one to be appointed an elder of a local church, when He says at verse 3:3, "not pugnacious," that is, not a brawler, as one always looking to start a fight with someone. So instead, God gives as a tenth and eleventh spiritual requirement that the man be "gentle" and "peaceable," which means caring for the thoughts and feelings of those one comes in contact with in order to maintain good human relations and stay on good terms with everyone. Let us note from Romans 12:18 what God's will is for believers in this regard, "If possible, so far as it depends on you, be at peace with all men." That is impossible if one is rude and aggressive in words and actions, and would certainly disqualify such a man from being considered as an overseer.

God goes on to a twelfth spiritual qualification at the end of verse 3:3, when He there says that for a man to be qualified to be an elder, he must be "free from the love of money." What this means is that one will not be seeking this position as a way to earn a living, as one would when one takes a job in the marketplace in order to pay the bills at home, for what is very important to see here is that this is God's spiritual work on earth, which is here in view, which means that those being raised for such a position are first of all being raised by God, for He has chosen these individuals in the first place, and since that is so, then God will ensure, as part of His provisions, that one is supplied in all needs, including financial, once one has been officially appointed to such a position!

Let us note what God later tells Timothy through the apostle Paul at 1 Timothy 6:9-11 in part, relating to this subject of "the love of money," [9] But those who want to get rich fall into temptation and a snare and many foolish and harmful desires which plunge men into ruin and destruction. [10] For the love of money is a root of all sorts of evil, and some by longing for it have wandered away from the faith and pierced themselves with many griefs. [11] But flee from these things, you man of God…" And so, that is why God says here, as a twelfth spiritual qualification for one to be appointed an elder, that one must already be "free from the love of money."

Then as a thirteenth spiritual qualification, God now brings in one's home life into the picture, when He goes on to say at verses 3:4,5, with the brackets at verse 5 being part of the Biblical text here, "[4] He must be one who manages his own household well, keeping his children under control with all dignity [5] (but if a man does not know how to manage his own household, how will he take care of the church of God?)." What this means then is that God regards the home as being the environment where a man, who is later earmarked by God to be raised by Him as an elder, will have honed the skills and principles in the physical everyday affairs of life that will later be useful in looking after the spiritual welfare of the believers, who are God's own children on earth! That is why God asks above, "if a man does not know how to manage his own household, HOW WILL HE TAKE CARE OF THE CHURCH OF GOD?"

What is interesting to note here is that God uses as a guidepost for "one who manages his own household well," as one who keeps "his children under control with all dignity," simply because God knows that the principle learnt here will be the same as when one is part of the oversight of the local church, which is God's own household. The key here to keeping "the children under control" is "with all dignity." When looking at that word "dignity" earlier at verse 2:2, we there said that it meant a way of living that showed a reverent life arising from one always taking the moral high ground, which would then be seen by all as an example to follow. What this means first in the home with the children, as it will be later in the local church with the believers, is that the head of the home, as will be true of those having the oversight, are there to model a Godly way of life that others can readily follow!

The goal here, in the home as in the local church, is to show forth to others that God is real, which will only occur as one lives a Godly life, which means showing forth the love of God to all one encounters, both in the way one talks with others and in the way one acts toward others! What this does is make others, first in the home and then in the local church, also want such a life, if one is not living such a life at that point. In a very real sense, the head of the home, as the one being part of the oversight of a local church, are only in that position as stewards of what rightly belongs to God, so that one is simply discharging one's spiritual duties under God as His representative in the sphere in which one has been appointed to by God!

Then we note that God continues at verse 3:6 and now does not give a spiritual qualification, but rather warns against appointing to the eldership "a new convert," with God's reason for doing so being, "so that he will not become conceited and fall into the condemnation incurred by the devil." In other words, a new believer would simply not yet be grounded in the faith, which means not only not yet having a good grasp of the truths of the faith in God's word, but also not yet having enough spiritual experience in living the Christian life so as to not be constantly led astray by some scheme of the devil, who has been practicing his evil craft since the time of Adam and Eve!

Just as it takes time for a man to grow from being a child into physical maturity, so too does it take time for a new believer to attain to a certain level of spiritual maturity, so as to start living in the will of God, instead of constantly living out of one's sinful nature. One good guide to know how far one has gone into spiritual maturity is to gauge how much one still falls prey in daily life to the three major sins that the devil likes to keep the whole of the human race in bondage to him with, which are pride, lust, and greed! God did not call the author as an evangelist until He had tested and approved me in all three of these areas, and I am convinced that this will also be the case with the calling of a man to be an elder of a local church, who will be gifted by God as either an evangelist or a shepherd/teacher! The devil knows that if he can lead the leadership of a local church astray, either through some sin or false teaching, then he will have a field day in scattering the flock, which is what God wants to avoid through this prohibition here!

Then as a fourteenth and final spiritual qualification, God goes on to say at verse 3:7 that the overseer "...must have a good reputation with those outside the church, so that he will not fall into reproach and the snare of the devil." It has never been easy to be a believer, even from the time of creation, for the first martyr in time was Abel, whom Cain, his brother, murdered. God gives us the reason for why Cain killed Abel at 1 John 3:12 in part, when He there says, "And for what reason did he slay him? Because his deeds were evil, and his brother's were righteous."

God is also aware that even as believers we are still indwelt of a sinful nature, which means that at times we might be tempted to compromise, especially when rubbing shoulders with unbelievers in the outside world, in order not to be persecuted for one's faith. This is why He warns believers at Galatians 1:10 in this regard, when He there says through the apostle Paul, "For do I now persuade men, or God? or do I seek to please men? for if I yet pleased men, I should not be the servant of Christ."

What this means then is that for a man, who is to be an elder in a local church, one must have a good reputation outside the church, and not just in the church, to show that one is not a hypocrite; that one has not compromised in regards to the truths of the faith and one is still living in accordance with the truth of God's word. What we need to realize as believers is that unbelievers can spot a phony faster than a believer at times, so that if one who is a true believer is not living in accordance with one's convictions, then that turns them off, and God cannot use one's witness to convict that person. While one may avoid being persecuted for the faith in compromising, yet at the same time one becomes as tasteless salt, as God describes at Matthew 5:13, "You are the salt of the earth; but if the salt has become tasteless, how can it be made salty again? It is no longer good for anything, except to be thrown out and trampled under foot by men."

What this means then is that if a man will not live for God, both before believers and unbelievers, then that man should not be appointed as an overseer as part of the oversight of a local church, for one is then prey to being accused of being a hypocrite and therefore casts a dark shadow on the rest of the local church believers in the eyes of unbelievers of that community. And if one compromises in one area of life, then the devil can easily use that to lead one to compromise also in other areas of life, so that as time goes on, not only that elder would have lost all credibility with the unbelievers there, but also the local church itself! That is why God wants to ensure that a man has a good reputation among unbelievers also, so that no one can accuse that man of anything after becoming an elder, which would then open the door for the devil to cause havoc for the believers of that local church through the failures of the one man!

1 Timothy 3:8-13, God's qualifications for the men who are to be deacons in a local church

After giving the spiritual qualifications for the men having the spiritual oversight of a local church at verses 3:1-7, God now goes on and gives the qualifications at 1 Timothy 3:8-13 required for those who would be appointed as deacons in a local church, as men who would now be under and assisting the elders in looking after the temporal affairs of the local church, *"[8] Deacons likewise must be men of dignity, not double-tongued, or addicted to much wine or fond of sordid gain, [9] but holding to the mystery of the faith with a clear conscience. [10] These men must also first be tested; then let them serve as deacons if they are beyond reproach. [11] Women must likewise be dignified, not malicious gossips, but temperate, faithful in all things. [12] Deacons must be husbands of only one wife, and good managers of their children and their own households. [13] For those who have served well as deacons obtain for themselves a high standing and great confidence in the faith that is in Christ Jesus."*

When God says here, "Deacons likewise must be," He is obviously indicating another group of men (since the word is plural), who are also appointed in the local church, apart from the elders, with God now going on to give the qualifications for these men before they are appointed. We clearly see the two groups of men mentioned together in the one local church at Philippi, when we read at Philippians 1:1, "Paul and Timothy, bond-servants of Christ Jesus, to all the saints (that is, all the believers) in Christ Jesus who are in Philippi, including the overseers and deacons:"

The word "deacons" simply indicates, in the present context, 'one who serves,' which in this case would be in direct service to the elders of the local church. So just as the elders look after the spiritual affairs of the local church, the deacons would look at the temporal, that is, the affairs of this life as they relate to that local church. God gives us an example of this division of labor between the spiritual and temporal in what He tells us at Acts 6:1-6, which was at Jerusalem, the first local church to be established on earth by God, "[1] Now at this time while the disciples were increasing in number, a complaint arose on the part of the Hellenistic Jews against the native Hebrews, because their widows were being overlooked in the daily serving of food. [2] So the twelve summoned the congregation of the disciples and said, "It is not desirable for us to neglect the word of God in order to serve tables. [3] Therefore, brethren, select from among you seven men of good reputation, full of the Spirit and of wisdom, whom we may put in charge of this task. [4] But we will devote ourselves to prayer and to the ministry of the word." [5] The statement found approval with the whole congregation; and they chose Stephen, a man full of faith and of the Holy Spirit, and Philip, Prochorus, Nicanor, Timon, Parmenas and Nicolas, a proselyte from Antioch. [6] And these they brought before the apostles; and after praying, they laid their hands on them."

When God goes on at verse 3:8 and says that deacons must be "men of dignity," we are to realize that this term is only one word in the original Greek, which simply means that one takes the work seriously and does it honorably. Then we note that in the rest of verse 3:8, God mentions three things that are negative in nature, which the local church needs to watch out for in appointing deacons – which appointment would indeed be done by the local church, this being based on what we see at Acts 6:2,3 quoted above.

And so, the first thing that a local church needs to ensure before appointing a man a deacon is that he is "not double-tongued," that is, one who says one thing to one person and something else to another, when speaking of the same thing. The second negative thing a local church is to watch out for is to ensure the man is not "addicted to much wine," where we now see that God here uses separate words and this is not all one term as it was at verse 3:3 for the overseer. And so, what is being said here is for a local church to watch if the man is given to, turns to, attends to, or gives himself to, much wine. This of course brings up the question of whether it is fine for him to drink wine, just as long as it is not "much"? Or is God saying here that the "much wine" involves using it for drinking also, apart from medicinal purposes?

Since we have concluded that the elders should be abstainers from all substances that would detract from one's walk with God by means of The Holy Spirit, then we would expect the same to be true for the deacons, for if they have a meal together, and one group is drinking wine and the other is not, then it would certainly place temptations before the abstainers that should not be there. And since we know for a fact that even one drink of alcohol alters one's physiological being, then one would think here that what God has in view at verse 3:8 is the appointment of deacons who in those days, when other medicines were not available, did use wine only for medicinal purposes, which would therefore mean that these would not be given to much wine, and would pass this part of the test as deacons.

Then the third thing that a local church was to watch out for was whether the man being considered as deacon was "fond of sordid gain" or not, where this whole term is only one word in the original Greek, meaning one who is not looking at making a fast buck by any means possible. For such a man would not be relying on God to supply all of one's needs, including financial, and would be a liability to the local church if appointed, in that he would be tempted by the devil whenever he handled church funds.

Then we see at verse 3:9 that in contrast to these three negative things, God now says that one positive qualification that one must have as a deacon is to be "holding to the mystery of the faith with a clear conscience." In other words, one must believe with conviction all the truth making up the faith we hold, and not just part of God's word. For if a man held to any teaching that was not of God, then it would be like inserting a sponge in a wall instead of a brick, and then expect the whole to hold together without eventually crumbling!

We then see that at verse 3:10, God says that a local church should first of all test "these men" – where this is only one word in the Greek, which again points to the fact that this is a male and not a female that God has in view here – with God not specifying the manner of the test, nor of the duration, leaving that to each local church to decide, but only making sure that the test does serve its purpose, which is to determine if one is suitable to be appointed as a deacon, as one who is beyond reproach (accusation) of any kind. For again, a deacon is still an appointed official of the local church and as such the man's character will reflect on the character and integrity of the whole group of believers making up that local church!

Then what is important to grasp when God continues at verse 3:11 and now says, "Women must likewise…," is that God has the wives of the men under consideration as deacons in view here. They "likewise," like their husband being considered as deacons must "be dignified, not malicious gossips, but temperate, faithful in all things." In God's sight, the man's wife is not a separate person from him, but rather "one flesh," as we have already noted. Therefore, the man appointed as deacon cannot be one thing and his wife another, for this will soon cause nothing but havoc in the local church, as for instance if the wife is not dignified, a malicious gossip, not temperate, and not faithful in all things!

God then reverts to speaking of the deacons again at verse 3:12, when He now brings in the man's home situation into the picture, as what also needs to be examined closely of one being considered for an appointment as a deacon in a local church. And so, as with the overseers, deacons must also be men of "one wife," who manage their children and households well. This therefore means these are men who hold to the institution of marriage, who are married and have children, which further means that they are older men. And since these men will be managing the temporal affairs of the local church, then it only stands to reason that their skills in those areas of life will have first been honed in the home, as what will later prove useful in the local church setting.

The reason that God includes the managing the children well here, as part of the requirements of one being appointed a deacon, is so that one will have gained sufficient maturity to handle the affairs of others. In other words, since children belong to God and a deacon is only a steward under God to deal with His temporal affairs of a local church, if one has not been faithful to Him in the home environment first, then how will he be in the local church? Also, raising children either matures one or breaks one, for the task requires one to move from being largely self-centered before marriage, then hopefully God-centered, and then other-centered, which will then bring about the proper management of the children and the home! And whatever is leaned here, in terms of gaining maturity, will no doubt prove useful in the local church, if one is appointed as a deacon.

What is interesting to then see is that at verse 3:13 God does NOT now give a qualification for one to have in order to become a deacon, but now instead concludes the matter in the sense of relating what a man will experience AFTER having served as deacon of a local church, in that those who are regarded by the local church as having served well as deacons will have a good standing in the eyes of all, in that they will have passed successfully through a threshold where one now holds a certain degree of influence in the local church. And as a result, one will have "great confidence in the faith that is in Christ Jesus," simply because one has been faithful in the position to which one was appointed in the local church, which was rendered in service to God and His people in a way that pleased God and therefore brings the blessing of God on one's life!

Before we go too far here, it should be noted that there is nothing stopping a deacon from later being appointed as an overseer in the local church, for some of the qualifications for the deacon are similar as for the appointment of an elder in the local church. For instance, in the passage at Acts 6:1-6 that we have looked at, we there see that

Philip was appointed as one of the men to serve food to the widows, which is a temporal task of a deacon, and yet later we see him as raised of God to preach the gospel, noting Acts 8:4-40, and later is referred to by God as an evangelist, noting Acts 21:8.

1 Timothy 3:14-16, God points out how one is to conduct oneself in the church, which is not only God's household, but also the pillar and support of the truth of the faith

As God brings this third chapter of His first letter to Timothy to a close, He now points out through the apostle Paul how one should conduct oneself as part of a local church while yet on earth, noting now what God says here at 1 Timothy 3:14-16, *"[14] I am writing these things to you, hoping to come to you before long; [15] but in case I am delayed, I write so that you will know how one ought to conduct himself in the household of God, which is the church of the living God, the pillar and support of the truth. [16] By common confession, great is the mystery of godliness: He who was revealed in the flesh, was vindicated in the Spirit, seen by angels, proclaimed among the nations, believed on in the world, taken up in glory."*

Here God leads the apostle Paul to write to Timothy that he is hoping to come to him soon at Ephesus, where Timothy still is, but in case he is delayed in getting there, Timothy ought to know how believers are to conduct themselves as part of the local church, which is regarded by God as "His household," in the sense that He indwells each one of the believers there by His Holy Spirit, with that local gathering of believers together being "the pillar and support of the truth," as where the truth of God's word is believed, being upheld, outworked, and made known in that locality.

Then God concludes at verse 3:16 by saying, "By common confession," that is, as what all believers should be able to attest to, "great is the mystery of godliness," in that great indeed is the truth that God revealed and has made known to mankind regarding what godliness is, in that God's Son, while on earth at His first coming from Heaven to earth, was the perfect embodiment of what Godliness is that God was making known to mankind in sending His precious Son to earth, which is then described by every step of His Son's life while here on earth in chronological order, as God continues here.

And so, speaking of God's Son when on earth at His first coming from Heaven to earth, God now declares, "He was revealed in the flesh," when He took on that body in the womb of the virgin that His Father had prepared for Him, noting Hebrews 10:5, so that when His Son was found in appearance as a Man, noting Philippians 2:8; He "was vindicated in the Spirit," meaning that He was declared to be Who He really was, namely The Son of God now in human flesh, noting Romans 1:3,4; He was "seen by angels," noting Luke 2:12,13; He was "proclaimed among the nations," noting Romans 16:25,26; He was "believed on in the world," noting 2 Thessalonians 1:9,10; and then at the time of His ascension, He was "taken up in glory," noting Acts 1:9-11.

CHAPTER FOUR

1 Timothy 4:1-16

1 Timothy 4:1-6, God warns Timothy that there is coming a time when some will fall away from the faith

As God begins this fourth chapter of His first letter to Timothy, He now warns Timothy that there is coming a time when some will fall away from the faith, noting what God here told him through the apostle Paul at 1 Timothy 4:1-5, *"[1] But the Spirit explicitly says that in later times some will fall away from the faith, paying attention to deceitful spirits and doctrines of demons, [2] by means of the hypocrisy of liars seared in their own conscience as with a branding iron, [3] (men) who forbid marriage and advocate abstaining from foods which God has created to be gratefully shared in by those who believe and know the truth. [4] For everything created by God is good, and nothing is to be rejected if it is received with gratitude; [5] for it is sanctified by means of the word of God and prayer. [6] In pointing out these things to the brethren, you will be a good servant of Christ Jesus, constantly nourished on the words of the faith and of the sound doctrine which you have been following."*

When the apostle Paul is led of God to write at verse 4:1, "But the Spirit explicitly says," he is referring to the fact that it was by The Holy Spirit indwelling in him that God The Father spoke to him and told him what he is about to disclose. Let us note what the apostle Paul was led of God to say at 2 Corinthians 13:3 in part, "…since you are seeking for proof of the Christ who speaks in me…," and also noting what God says of believers in general at Matthew 10:20, "For it is not you who speak, but it is the Spirit of your Father who speaks in you." The word "explicitly" here means that this was expressed in definite terms, as something that is sure to occur.

And what was sure to occur was "that in later times some will fall away from the faith..." The term "later times" here, which is two words in the original Greek, speaks of a definite period of time that God has in view and which He is disclosing in this letter to Timothy. It is important to keep in mind that God has the end of the present third age of time in view here, as something that will occur in every local church on a worldwide scale.

What we will see occur, which we are seeing in our day, because we are now in the end time of the present third age, is that "some will fall away from the faith..." The term "fall away" here is but one word in the Greek, which could also have been rendered as 'depart from, turn away from, and apostatize.' When God speaks of a falling away from the faith, He does not mean that true believers will suddenly become unbelievers, which is an impossibility, but rather, what is in view here is people only professing to be believers, who are attending a local church with true believers, will suddenly leave the faith that they once only professed, but were never truly a part of!

God also speaks of this exact same time period and occurrence when He goes on to say at 1 John 2:18-20, "[18] Children, it is the last hour; and just as you heard that antichrist is coming, even now many antichrists have appeared; from this we know that it is the last hour. [19] They went out from us, but they were not really of us; for if they had been of us, they would have remained with us; but they went out, so that it would be shown that they all are not of us. [20] But you have an anointing from the Holy One, and you all know."

There are three very important truths that God tells us in these verses. The first is that there is a person coming on the world scene in time, who will be called, "antichrist." Secondly, God tells us that even now, during the present third age of time, there are "many antichrists," not meaning here that the one who will eventually have that title has appeared, but rather that there are many human beings now on earth, who exhibit the same characteristics that this person, who will the antichrist, will himself exhibit when he does appear on the world scene!

Then the third very important truth that God makes known to us is that it is now "the last hour," speaking here of the end of the present third age. In other words, the present age is just on the verge of ending, with very little time left. And the reason that God gives for our knowing that it is "the last hour," is that "many antichrists have appeared." In other words, just from the fact that so many people the world over oppose God's eternal Son, The Lord Jesus Christ, is proof that we are very close to the end of the present third age of time!

Then in the rest of 1 Timothy 4:1 and at verse 2 and 3, God tells us 'how' those mere professors of the faith will fall away, as those that will depart from among the believers, which will be because of "the hypocrisy of liars," which are human unbelievers, who have their consciences seared "as with a branding iron." This simply means that they have sinned so often that their conscience – which God gives all human beings born into this world, in order to discern good and evil – no longer responds at all to what is good and of God, only responding to what is evil and of the devil, which further means that their conscience has now been hardened, so that it will now no longer ever respond to what is good as a judgment from God!

That is why these unbelieving "liars" will be tools of "deceitful spirits," which are fallen angels, also referred to as 'evil or unclean spirits' and 'demons' in God's word, and will therefore be teaching "doctrines of demons" to those who are mere professors of the faith, thereby causing them to fall away, that is, to depart from among the believers. These unbelievers will be believing these teachings from the pit of hell as a judgment from God, because "the later times" will have now arrived in God's timing of events, as a time as we are now seeing when evil is so prevalent in the world that only true believers will go on in a walk with God until the end of the age, and that as a work of God's grace and power alone!

The word "men" has been placed in brackets here at verse 4:3, because this is an added word by the translators from the original Greek into English. The reality is that both men and women unbelievers will be tools of the devil in the last days of the present third age of time, as those who will "forbid marriage" and teach others to abstain from certain foods. The reason they will forbid marriage is because they oppose what God instituted, which is marriage, which God wants all human beings to honor, noting Hebrews 13:4.

And the reason they want people to abstain from certain foods is due to the fact that "God has created (all, including food) to be gratefully shared in by those who believe and know the truth (that is, all true believers), because these are aware that "everything created by God is good, and nothing is to be rejected if received with gratitude, (because) it is sanctified by means of the word of God and prayer." In other words, God has not only declared all food "clean" in His word (noting Mark 7:19; Acts 10:14,15), but when we give thanks for the food we eat, we are acknowledging that the food we are about to eat comes from His bountiful supply to us, as His provision to strengthen us physically in His service while on earth, carrying out His will for our lives all for His glory!

So God tells Timothy at verse 4:6 to keep telling the believers the truth of what He has just disclosed to him at verses 4:1-5, doing so there at Ephesus and wherever God might have him in the future, for in doing so, he will show himself to be a faithful "servant of Christ Jesus," as one who is constantly being "nourished on the words of the faith," as found in God's word, and which now makes up the "sound teaching," which he himself has been personally following so far.

1 Timothy 4:7-11, God counsels Timothy to discipline himself for the purpose of godliness and to teach others to do the same

As God continues to teach Timothy through the apostle Paul, we now see from 1 Timothy 4:7-11 that He now counsels Timothy to discipline himself for the purpose of godliness and to teach others to do the same, noting now what we there read, *"[7] But have nothing to do with worldly fables fit only for old women. On the other hand, discipline yourself for the purpose of godliness; [8] for bodily discipline is only of little profit, but godliness is profitable for all things, since it holds promise for the present life and also for the life to come. [9] It is a trustworthy statement deserving full acceptance. [10] For it is for this we labor and strive, because we have fixed our hope on the living God, who is the Savior of all men, especially of believers. [11] Prescribe and teach these things."*

God begins here by pointing out to Timothy that godliness is what he is to lead a disciplined life in order to achieve, but he is to watch out for what was a common occurrence at Ephesus, which was for people there to be occupied with "worldly fables," that is, to what was opposite to the truth as found in God's word. The word rendered "fables" here was rendered as "myths" at verse 1:4 earlier. The fact that the apostle Paul is led of God to say "worldly fables fit only for old women" here more than likely meant that these were the prime spreaders of these "worldly fables" among the people there! We can be sure that God has nothing against "old women" here!

When God talks of "godliness" at verse 4:7 – which is the same word as used at verse 3:16, where God pointed out that His Son, The Lord Jesus Christ, was the embodiment of godliness, when here on earth in human likeness at His first coming from Heaven – God is speaking of a holy life lived for the purpose of accomplishing His will while here on earth, as what brings pleasure to His heart. It is a life that will be lived when one is living by God's imparted righteous life (that is, His righteousness) moment by moment, with no known unconfessed sins in one's life. Timothy was already well on his way to godliness, as he was, as we have seen at verse 4:6, constantly nourishing himself on the words of the faith and its sound teaching as found in God's word.

God also touches on this godliness when He counsels all believers at Romans 12:1,2, by there saying, "[1] Therefore I urge you, brethren, by the mercies of God, to present your bodies a living and holy sacrifice, acceptable to God, which is your spiritual service of worship. [2] And do not be conformed to this world, but be transformed by the renewing of your mind, so that you may prove what the will of God is, that which is good and acceptable and perfect," and also at Romans 14:17,18, "[17] for the kingdom of God is not eating and drinking, but righteousness and peace and joy in the Holy Spirit. [18] For he who in this way serves Christ is acceptable to God and approved by men."

As God goes on to point out at 1 Timothy 4:8, "bodily discipline" – such as early to bed, early to rise, proper nutrition, and adequate exercise – is of some profit to be sure, but will never achieve what godliness will achieve for any human being. For what we need to ever remember is that bodily discipline is only for this life, and only concerns the physical aspect of mankind, while godliness, on the other hand, has value, not only in this life, but also in the life to come, after our course on earth has reached its end. One who is a believer only needs to imagine what a life without God is like, which is a miserable life in contrast to the peace, the joy, the love of God that one experiences on a moment-by-moment basis, as one walks with God by His imparted life with no known unconfessed sins in one's life!

Godliness being experienced now is but a foretaste of what life will be like when we are in God's Presence forever in Heaven! And so, that is why God tells Timothy at verse 4:10,11 that what He has just said to him regarding godliness, in terms of its value for one who is a true believer – is "a trustworthy statement deserving full acceptance" by all believers, and so is something that Timothy was to instruct and teach other believers there about, where he was at Ephesus.

1 Timothy 4:12-16, personal instructions that God gives to Timothy, but which all believers would benefit from

At 1 Timothy 4:12-16, we now have personal instructions that God led the apostle Paul to give to Timothy, which were to be applied to his own life, but which all believers can benefit in also applying to one's life, noting now what God there said, *"[12] Let no one look down on your youthfulness, but rather in speech, conduct, love, faith and purity, show yourself an example of those who believe. [13] Until I come, give attention to the (public) reading (of Scripture), to exhortation and teaching. [14] Do not neglect the spiritual gift within you, which was bestowed on you through prophetic utterance with the laying on of hands by the presbytery. [15] Take pains with these things; be absorbed in them, so that your progress will be evident to all. [16] Pay close attention to yourself and to your teaching; persevere in these things, for as you do this you will ensure salvation both for yourself and for those who hear you."*

We are to note that the likely reason that God begins by saying to Timothy, "Let no one look down on your youthfulness," was due to the fact that Timothy was younger than the apostle Paul and the other men that we traveling with him, who were all older men, and not that Timothy was necessarily that young. Another term which could have been applied here is 'youthful age.' And so, as a result, he was not to let those he was to minister to despise or slight the fact that he was younger than the others.

Let us note for instance what God led the apostle Paul to write to the local church at Corinth in regards to Timothy at 1 Corinthians 16:10,11, "[10] Now if Timothy comes, see that he is with you without cause to be afraid, for he is doing the Lord's work, as I also am. [11] So let no one despise him. But send him on his way in peace, so that he may come to me; for I expect him with the brethren." God likely wrote this to Timothy here because his being younger than the others was affecting his ministry and now God was specifically dealing with it.

As God continues here, he then leads the apostle Paul to say to Timothy in the rest of verse 4:12 to not dwell on the fact that he was younger than the others, but instead he was to show himself an example to those he came in contact with, who were believers, doing so in the way he spoke, in the way he lived, in showing forth the love of God and his faith in Him, as one not having any known unconfessed sins in his life!

As we then see at verse 4:13, Timothy's main task in ministry while at Ephesus was "to give attention to the (public) reading (of Scripture), to exhortation and teaching," In other words, he was being directed by God to attend to – in the sense of putting all his thoughts and efforts into – the reading of God's word, when gathered with believers in a public way, then he was to encourage the believers to live in accordance with God's word that was read, while instructing the believers on the meaning of the text of Gods word being read. What we have here then is God's way for one called into ministry to handle God's word when gathered in a public way with those who are believers!

Then at verse 4:14, when God says to Timothy, "Do not neglect the spiritual gift within you, which was bestowed on you through prophetic utterance with the laying on of hands by the presbytery," God is simply reminding Timothy of the spiritual gift that he now had from Him, which was the gift of evangelism, which was given to him at the same time that God had a New Testament prophet utter a prophetic utterance, while the elders of the local church he was a part of laid their hands on him. Later, at 2 Timothy 1:6, we there see God lead the apostle Paul to again remind Timothy of that same occurrence, as we there read, "For this reason I remind you to kindle afresh the gift of God which is in you through the laying on of my hands." What is in view here is that God gave the gift of evangelism to Timothy at the time when Paul and the elders of the local church at Lystra laid hands on him, which spoke of their confirmation of this, in the sense that God would have confirmed the giving of the gift of evangelism to Timothy in their spirit by The Holy Spirit indwelling there.

We are to note that at Ephesians 3:6,7, God gives us an example of this when He there leads Paul to speak of the gift of apostleship that he received from God as a work of His grace alone for him to preach the gospel, "[6] …to be specific, that the Gentiles are fellow heirs and fellow members of the body, and fellow partakers of the promise in Christ Jesus through THE GOSPEL, [7] OF WHICH I WAS MADE A MINISTER, ACCORDING TO THE GIFT OF GOD'S GRACE WHICH WAS GIVEN TO ME ACCORDING TO THE WORKING OF HIS POWER." The only difference in Timothy's case here at verse 4:14 is that he was being gifted as an evangelist to preach the exact same gospel of God's Son that Paul had been gifted by God to preach as an apostle!

All of this at verse 4:14 would have taken place when the apostle Paul was at Timothy's local church at Lystra in Galatia and wanted to take Timothy along as part of his ministry team, as led of God for him to do so, noting again Acts 16:1-3 here that we earlier looked at, but now in order to refresh our memories, "[1] Paul came also to Derbe and to Lystra. And a disciple was there, named Timothy, the son of a Jewish woman who was a believer, but his father was a Greek, [2] and he was well spoken of by the brethren who were in Lystra and Iconium. [3] Paul wanted this man to go with him; and he took him and circumcised him because of the Jews who were in those parts, for they all knew that his father was a Greek."

God gives us a Biblical example at Acts 13 of what we see occurring at 1 Timothy 4:14, when God bestowed the gift of apostleship on both Paul (who was at that time still Saul) and Barnabas, as we now see from Acts 13:1-4, "[1] Now there were at Antioch, in the church that was there, prophets and teachers: Barnabas, and Simeon who was called Niger, and Lucius of Cyrene, and Manaen who had been brought up with Herod the tetrarch, and Saul. [2] While they were ministering to the Lord and fasting, the Holy Spirit said, "Set apart for Me Barnabas and Saul for the work to which I have called them." [3] Then, when they had fasted and prayed and laid their hands on them, they sent them away. [4] So, being sent out by the Holy Spirit, they went down to Seleucia and from there they sailed to Cyprus."

What is instructive for us to note here is that there were five men gathered in prayer at the local church at Antioch in Syria, which was no doubt the leaders of the local church, these being those raised of God as its elders, this being, we must remember, during the foundation stage of the present third age, noting Ephesians 2:20. And what is also instructive for us to see here is that these five men – and it is important to also note that they were indeed all men – are identified here by what they did in the local church at Antioch, being told here that they were "prophets and teachers." Then we note that while they were all in prayer, two of the five men, namely Barnabas and Saul, were chosen by God The Father through His Son, The Lord Jesus Christ, by The Holy Spirit, and then sent out from the local church, then being told that they went to Cyprus from Antioch.

And what we further need to observe here is that the three men who remained at Antioch were the New Testament "prophets" here, later to be seen as the shepherd/teachers of Ephesians 4:11, after the close of the canon of the New Testament Scriptures; while Barnabas and Saul, who were the two men sent out here, were the "teachers" mentioned at verse 13:1. And what is further instructive to note is that at Acts 13:9, Saul is henceforth referred to as "Paul" by God and then at Acts 14:14, we have both Paul and Barnabas now referred to by God as 'apostles,' which simply means 'one sent forth,' noting what we there read, "But when THE APOSTLES Barnabas and Paul heard of it, they tore their robes and rushed out into the crowd, crying out..." And so, we see that Barnabas and Paul, who were previously identified as "teachers" before they were sent out from the local church at Antioch, are now called "apostles," after they have been sent out by God!

What is also important to note from this passage at Acts 13 is that God would have communicated to each of the five elders in prayer what He was in the process of doing here, which is clear from verse 13:2, where we read, "While they were ministering to the Lord and fasting, the Holy Spirit said, "Set apart for Me Barnabas and Saul for the work to which I have called them." And as a result of God speaking to these men there in leadership, regarding what He was in the process of doing with Barnabas and Saul, then the other three men now lay their hands on both Barnabas and Saul, as we see at verse 13:3, "Then, when they had fasted and prayed and laid their hands on them, they sent them away," with the laying on of hands here simply meaning two things. The first being that they were all in agreement with what was being done, and secondly, that they would be supporting these two being sent out, doing so in prayer and in whatever other way might be necessary in their gospel ministry, such as their financial needs. We need to keep in mind that after the canon of the New Testament had been given by God, apostles were then called "evangelists" and the prophets became "shepherd/teachers," this then continuing on and being the case to the end of the present third age.

In regards to a prophetic utterance, which we see mentioned as relating to Timothy at 1 Timothy 4:14, we are to see a Biblical example of this, which God made to the apostle Paul at the time that he was saved by God, noting what we read at Acts 26:16-18, "[16] 'But get up and stand on your feet; for this purpose I have appeared to you, to appoint you a minister and a witness not only to the things which you have seen, but also to the things in which I will appear to you; [17] rescuing you from the Jewish people and from the Gentiles, to whom I am sending you, [18] to open their eyes so that they may turn from darkness to light and from the dominion of Satan to God, that they may receive forgiveness of sins and an inheritance among those who have been sanctified by faith in Me.' Only later, as we saw at Acts 13:1-4, did this become a reality for Paul, which was when God gifted him and Barnabas as apostles, and sent them forth.

The only difference now, as relating to Timothy, is that God did not make that prophetic utterance directly to him, as He had done with the apostle Paul at Acts 26, but rather now spoke through one of the elders, who would have been a prophet in the local church at Lystra, when the apostle Paul was there and wanted to take Timothy along as part of his gospel ministry team, which was God's will for him to do, and which is when God gifted Timothy as an evangelist. We are not told what that "prophetic utterance" was that was made as relating to Timothy. And if we recall what was earlier said of Timothy at verse 1:18, namely, "This command I entrust to you, Timothy, my son, in accordance with THE PROPHECIES PREVIOUSLY MADE CONCERNING YOU, that by them you fight the good fight," it would appear that other prophecies were also made relating to Timothy, but not recorded either.

Then, as we see from verses 4:15, God continues giving Timothy personal instructions in carrying out his ministry there at Ephesus, now saying to him, "Take pains with these things; be absorbed in them," He wants Timothy to attend to these things by making them the central focus of his ministry, for then, as God continues, "so that your progress will be evident to all," so that it will be seen by all that he was personally growing, not only in the faith, but in spiritual maturity in a way that would be noticeable to those he would be coming in contact with there at Ephesus.

When God goes on at verse 4:16 and says to Timothy, "Pay close attention to yourself and to your teaching," He wants to make Timothy aware that his life will affect his teaching, as part of his evangelistic ministry. He cannot teach to others what he is not practicing in his own life. His talk must match his walk and vice versa. What he is in himself will be reflected in what comes out of his mouth, which is why God says at Matthew 12:34, "You brood of vipers, how can you, being evil, speak what is good? For the mouth speaks out of that which fills the heart."

So then God continues and says to Timothy in the rest of verse 4:16 that once your life and your teaching are on the right track, in terms of your life being one that is pleasing to God, which also means one's teaching ministry to others will be effective, then "persevere in these things, for as you do this you will ensure salvation both for yourself and for those who hear you." In other words, as you persevere living a life pleasing to God, He will not only bless you with an effective ministry, but the end result will be that not only your soul will be saved, but also those to whom God leads you to minister to! This is the ultimate reward for faithful service to God.

CHAPTER FIVE

1 Timothy 5:1-25

1 Timothy 5:1,2, God's instructions to Timothy regarding older men and women, and younger men and women

As God begins this fifth chapter of His first letter to Timothy, we note that He now gives him instructions regarding how to best deal with the older folks and the younger folks of both genders he would be coming in contact with in his ministry, as we now see from 1 Timothy 5:1,2, *"[1] Do not sharply rebuke an older man, but rather appeal to him as a father, to the younger men as brothers, [2] the older women as mothers, and the younger women as sisters, in all purity."*

It is clear from what God says to Timothy here that He regards the spiritual family of God on earth as if it were one's own family in the physical realm, which meant that Timothy was to ensure he did not speak harshly to a man older than himself, but rather was to encourage such men by way of God's word, also speaking with the males younger than himself as he would to his own younger brother in the flesh; also speaking to the older women as he would to his own mother; and to the younger women as he would to his own sister, while at the same time keeping his thoughts and his gaze pure in his dealings with them, so as to be careful not to be led into sin.

1 Timothy 5:3-16, God's instructions to Timothy regarding those women he would be coming in contact with who were widows

As God continues, it is clear from what He now instructs Timothy at 1 Timothy 5:3-16 that He has a tender spot in His heart for those women who were widows. So let us note to begin with what God says to Timothy at 1 Timothy 5:3-8 regarding widows, *"[3] Honor widows who are widows indeed; [4] but if any widow has children or grandchildren, they must first learn to practice piety in regard to their own family and to make some return to their parents; for this is acceptable in the sight of God. [5] Now she who is a widow indeed and who has been left alone, has fixed her hope on God and continues in entreaties and prayers night and day. [6] But she who gives herself to wanton pleasure is dead even while she lives. [7] Prescribe these things as well, so that they may be above reproach. [8] But if anyone does not provide for his own, and especially for those of his household, he has denied the faith and is worse than an unbeliever."*

And so, we see that God begins here and says to Timothy to "Honor widows who are widows indeed," which meant to hold in high regard and to materially assist women who found themselves in that situation, further noting here that God then defines at verse 5:5 the widows that He regarded as being widows worthy of honor and assistance, "Now she who is a widow indeed and who has been left alone, has fixed her hope on God and continues in entreaties and prayers night and day."

In other words, a woman might have been left alone, in terms of her husband having died leaving her without support, but if she is not the kind of widow who is first of all trusting God to meet all of her needs, which will be shown by the life of faith that she lives, including her prayer life, in terms of what she is praying for, then she is not the type of widow that believers should be holding in high regard and materially assisting. For as God says at verse 5:4, the first responsibility in the care of widows falls to one's own family, so that if a widow has children or grandchildren, then these should be materially assisting their mother or grandmother who is a widow, before that responsibility falls to the local church, who can then concentrate on those widows as God describes at verse 5:5, whose only hope for support is God!

When God says at verse 5:3 that family members "must first learn to practice piety in regard to their own family," He is saying that in fulfilling one's duty to one's family member, as for instance caring for a mother or grandmother who is a widow, one is showing one's reverence for God, Who delights in such actions, noting for instance what He tells us at Hebrews 6:10, "For God is not unjust so as to forget your work and the love which you have shown toward His name, in having ministered and in still ministering to the saints." As God goes on to point out at verse 5:8, as now a general principle to keep in mind, He regards as an unbeliever, as one without faith in God, who refuses to help a member of one's family, especially if the one in need is of one's own household!

The kind of widows that God points out as not being worthy of honor or of material assistance were those He describes at verse 5:6, as "she who gives herself to wanton pleasure is dead even while she lives." In other words, widows who only live to satisfy their own carnal desires, instead of living so as to please God, were to be regarded as being dead spiritually, that is, dead to life with God, even though still alive physically!

Then at 1 Timothy 5:9-16, God continues to instruct Timothy in regards to widows he might encounter in his ministry, mentioning those which the local church was to materially assist, and also those the local church was not to materially assist, noting now what God there says, *"[9] A widow is to be put on the list only if she is not less than sixty years old, having been the wife of one man, [10] having a reputation for good works; and if she has brought up children, if she has shown hospitality to strangers, if she has washed the saints' feet, if she has assisted those in distress, and if she has devoted herself to every good work. [11] But refuse to put younger widows on the list, for when they feel sensual desires in disregard of Christ, they want to get married, [12] thus incurring condemnation, because they have set aside their previous pledge. [13] At the same time they also learn to be idle, as they go around from house to house; and not merely idle, but also gossips and busybodies, talking about things not proper to mention. [14] Therefore, I want younger widows to get married, bear children, keep house, and give the enemy no occasion for reproach; [15] for some have already turned aside to follow Satan. [16] If any woman who is a believer has dependent widows, she must assist them and the church must not be burdened, so that it may assist those who are widows indeed."*

We see God begin at verse 5:9 by instructing Timothy about keeping a list of widows for the local church there at Ephesus to materially assist, which reminds us of the mention of widows that we earlier encountered at Acts 6, when discussing the deacons in chapter three, noting again what we read at Acts 6:1-3 for our present purpose, "[1] Now at this time while the disciples were increasing in number, a complaint arose on the part of the Hellenistic Jews against the native Hebrews, because their widows were being overlooked in the daily serving of food. [2] So the twelve summoned the congregation of the disciples and said, "It is not desirable for us to neglect the word of God in order to serve tables. [3] "Therefore, brethren, select from among you seven men of good reputation, full of the Spirit and of wisdom, whom we may put in charge of this task." What this means then, for our present purpose, is that it would be up to the deacons of the local church to not only make up such a list of widows that needed material assistance, based on God's conditions at verses 5:9,10, but it was also the deacon's duty to ensure that they were provided for as God directed in accordance with the needs in each case.

God then continues at verses 5:9 to now give conditions that needed to be met by a widow before she was added to such a list, that would then result in her being materially assisted by the local church. The first condition to be met was that a widow needed to be sixty years and above. The second condition was that a widow was to have "been the wife of one man," in terms of not being a woman who had been divorced and remarried and then finding herself a widow. When we looked at the qualifications for an overseer earlier, we saw at verse 3:2 that God there specified that he had to be "the husband of one wife," where we also there stated that this referred to him as not being a divorced and remarried man. It is important to ever remember that with God, there is no divorce once married, with only the death of either spouse annulling the marriage. This of course means that the remarriage of a divorced person would also not be of God.

Then God's third condition for a widow to be placed on the local church list for assistance was that she needed to have "a reputation for good works," that is, those who know this widow must be able to testify, to report, that she indeed does things that are of worth and honorable. What needs to be ensured here is that after a widow has been placed on the list for assistance that no one will be able to criticize the local church for having that widow on the list, which means that she must be above reproach in how she lives.

God's fourth condition is that she needs to have "brought up children," where the term "brought up children" is but one word in the original Greek, which speaks of her having reared children that were hers, as a mother. It is important to keep in mind here that God places a high value on motherhood, and that the opening of the womb in order for a woman to conceive, or the closing the womb to prevent her from conceiving, is always seen to be in the Hands of God in Scripture, so that when a woman pleases God in the way she lives, she will be enabled of God to have children, and when she does not please God in the way she lives, then He will prevent her from conceiving a child. What this means for our present context then is that if a widow has "brought up children," then it means that she lived in a way that pleased God, Who opened her womb to conceive and bear those children! Please note carefully what we read in God's word at Genesis 4:1; 21:1,2; 30:21,22; 1 Samuel 1:1-11,19,20; and 2 Samuel 6:20-23.

Then Gods' fifth condition, also at verse 5:10, was for a widow to have "shown hospitality to strangers," which means that her home, while her husband was alive, was one where "strangers" were welcomed, which further means that this shows that she was willing to care for the less fortunate and the sojourners among them, because the burden of such hospitality in one's home would have fallen mostly on her shoulders! We know that hospitality is something that God desires believers to practice, as we have also seen from verse 3:2 that God even made it one of the spiritual qualifications for one to be considered as an overseer in a local church.

A sixth condition that God goes on to mention at verse 5:10 is that a widow "washed the saints' feet." What would be in view here is being willing to humble herself when a guest entered one's home, since the most common footwear worn in those days were open toe sandals, and since most of the roads were dusty, this meant that when one entered a person's home, one would remove one's sandals at the door, at which point someone in the home, which in this case would be the widow who had been a wife, would wash a person's feet and dry them before proceeding barefoot in the home. It was also customary to provide some olive oil for one's face due to the drying effect of the hot Middle Eastern sun, noting here Luke 7:44-46 and John 13:3-5.

Then God goes on to a seventh condition at verse 5:10, which is that for a widow to be placed on the list of those receiving material assistance from the local church she must first "have assisted those in distress," which would show that she had compassion for others in their time of need, as she was now herself needing compassion from others in her time of need! As God says at Luke 6:38 in part, "For by your standard of measure it will be measured to you in return." God sees all and remembers all that we say, do, and think, and He rewards in kind, which is why He says a few verses before at Luke 6:31, "Treat others the same way you want them to treat you."

Then God's eighth and last condition for a widow to be placed on the list for assistance is for her to have "devoted herself to every good work." In God's third condition at the start of verse 5:10, we there learned that a widow needed to have "a reputation for good works," where the focus was on others being able to testify to her "good works," where the word "good" is the Greek word "Kalos," and speaking of what would be considered as right, noble, and honorable in God's sight; for if God is satisfied with one's good works, then believers here on earth should be also!

And now in this eighth condition, when here speaking of "good works," the word "works" is the same as at the third condition, but here the word "good' is the Greek word "Agathos," speaking of what is beneficial in its effect. So when God says here as an eighth condition that a widow needs to have "devoted herself to every good work," He is speaking of the fact that she needs to have followed after the good works that are part of God's will for believers as children of God. At Ephesians 2:10, God tells us the following, "For we (as believers) are His workmanship, created in Christ Jesus (at the moment of our salvation) for good works (same two words as the eighth condition above), which God prepared beforehand so that we would walk in them." When looking at verse 2:10 earlier, we were there told in regards to believing women, adding verse 9 for context, "[9] Likewise, I want women to adorn themselves with proper clothing, modestly and discreetly, not with braided hair and gold or pearls or costly garments, [10] but rather by means of good works, as is proper for women making a claim to godliness," where again the words "good works" are the same as at the eighth condition above."

Then starting at verse 5:11, God now goes on to tell Timothy that there are certain widows that would not be suitable for including on a list for assistance by the local church, with those automatically excluded would be the "younger widows," which were defined by God at verse 5:9 as being those less than sixty years of age, with God giving His reason for doing so in the rest of verse 5:11 and 5:12, when He says, "...for when they feel sensual desires in disregard of Christ, they want to get married, thus incurring condemnation, because they have set aside their previous pledge." What is important to see here is that the whole phrase in English, "feel sensual desires in disregard," is only ONE word in the original Greek, which speaks of becoming 'wanton.'

The thought then, and speaking here of a widow who is a believer, is that she is in the process of having desires that one requires a man to fulfill, which leads her to have thoughts that are more on marriage than on serving God's Son, The Lord Jesus Christ, Whom she was free to serve wholeheartedly when she first became a widow. And as such, because her thoughts are off God's Son, she is in danger of becoming immoral and of incurring God's judgment, as what would result if she did become immoral.

It is for this reason that God leads the apostle Paul to write at verse 5:14,15 here, "Therefore, I want younger widows to get married, bear children, keep house, and give the enemy no occasion for reproach; for some have already turned aside to follow Satan." It would indeed be a reproach to the cause of Christ on earth if a believer, such as a younger widow here in view, became immoral, that is, fell into the sin of fornication, which is sex outside of marriage. If that happened, then one would indeed "have already turned aside to follow Satan," in that one would have given in to the temptation that would have come from the devil.

God is very much aware of the weakness of man's flesh and of the sin of immorality, as He leads the apostle Paul to also write at 1 Corinthians 7:2,5 "[2] But because of immoralities, each man is to have his own wife, and each woman is to have her own husband... [5] Stop depriving one another (as husband and wife), except by agreement for a time, so that you may devote yourselves to prayer, and come together again SO THAT SATAN WILL NOT TEMPT YOU BECAUSE OF YOUR LACK OF SELF-CONTROL.

Not only were the younger widows in danger of falling into the sin of immorality, but as God points out at verse 5:13, He was also aware of other dangers for them, as He points out here through the apostle Paul, "At the same time they also learn to be idle, as they go around from house to house; and not merely idle, but also gossips and busybodies, talking about things not proper to mention." The word "idle" here refers to a one who is inactive, unfruitful, not only in the things of God, which means that one is not walking with God, but also in terms of leading a useful life in general. And when a believer is in that unfortunate situation, then we can be sure that the devil will find things for one to do, which will obviously have nothing to do with God, as we see from what God mentions here, even to lead one into an immoral life if one persists in not walking with God.

If one is truly a believer in such a state, then God will eventually intervene with his judgment, in that something will happen as He seeks to bring that person to their senses, noting for instance what God mentions at 1 Corinthians 11:30-32, "[30] For this reason many among you are WEAK AND SICK, AND A NUMBER SLEEP (that is, have died). [31] But if we judged ourselves rightly, we would not be judged. [32] But when we are judged, we are DISCIPLINED BY THE LORD so that we will not be condemned along with the world" (in the final judgment of time).

And so, God concludes the matter in regards to widows by saying to Timothy at verse 5:16, "If any woman who is a believer has dependent widows (that is, a mother or grandmother who needs assistance), she must assist them and the church must not be burdened, so that it may assist those who are widows indeed," as defined by God at verses 5:9,10. We note from what God says here that He places the responsibility for caring for a widow on the believing women in the widow's family, whether that be a daughter, a granddaughter, or a sister of the widow. Two likely reasons here are that a woman can best help another woman, since being a woman one understands what another woman is undergoing in thoughts and feelings; and secondly, a widow would be in a vulnerable state, as we have seen, and the last thing that she needs at this point is for a man to be providing for her assistance. That would only be opening a door for the devil to work.

1 Timothy 5:17-22, God's instructions to Timothy regarding the elders of the local church

From the instructions that we now see God give Timothy at 1 Timothy 5:17-22, regarding the elders of the local church, it is obvious that what was said earlier at verse 3:1-7 regarding the overseers was indeed a reference to the elders of the local church, since the word "elders" is simply another term for the men in leadership who have the oversight of the local church under God. And so, as we see here, God also has instructions for Timothy regarding these elders, since Timothy as an evangelist would have ministered the gospel at Ephesus for two years with the apostle Paul, and would now be in a position to appoint the elders of the local church there at Ephesus, now having the qualifications of verses 3:1-7 to guide him.

And so, God's further instructions to him regarding elders are as we see at 1 Timothy 5:17-22, *"[17] The elders who rule well are to be considered worthy of double honor, especially those who work hard at preaching and teaching. [18] For the Scripture says, "You shall not muzzle the ox while he is threshing," and "The laborer is worthy of his wages." [19] Do not receive an accusation against an elder except on the basis of two or three witnesses. [20] Those who continue in sin, rebuke in the presence of all, so that the rest also will be fearful of sinning. [21] I solemnly charge you in the presence of God and of Christ Jesus and of His chosen angels, to maintain these principles without bias, doing nothing in a spirit of partiality. [22] Do not lay hands upon anyone too hastily and thereby share responsibility for the sins of others; keep yourself free from sin."*

There are four instructions that God gives Timothy regarding the elders here, which are meant to be taken in by believers in local churches everywhere. The first is at verses 5:17,18; the second at verses 5:19,20; the third at verse 5:21; and the fourth at verse 5:22. When God begins His first instruction by saying, "The elders who rule well," He is making reference to those men who have the oversight of the local church and as such preside over and lead the believers there in a right, noble, and honorable way under God. Such elders are to be "considered worthy of double honor," that is, should be deemed as deserving a twofold valuation, both tangible and intangible, in terms of proper remuneration and the respect and high regard they should be held in by all the believers of that local church.

When God adds, "especially those who work hard at preaching and teaching," He is indicating a certain situation here in that in a small congregation of believers, there might be only two elders, one being an evangelist and the other a shepherd/teacher, so that one would be doing the preaching, where the focus is on God's Son, The Lord Jesus Christ, so that the believers have a clear conception of the gospel and are able to share it with others and so see the local church grow numerically; and the other, the teaching, where the focus is on the doctrines of God's word, so that the believers might grow to spiritual maturity in the faith as they practice these truths in their own lives.

However, in a large congregation of believers, there might be three, four, five, six, or more elders, and whereas these would be gifted as either evangelists or shepherd/teachers, yet at times some of the elders might be found to be more proficient than the others at preaching and teaching so that the task would fall mainly to them. For instance, some of the elders might have been believers longer than some of the others and might have a better grasp of the Scriptures. So here at verse 5:17, God is indicating that those elders who carry most of the load of preaching and teaching among the elders should especially be considered of double honor!

At verse 5:18, God simply quotes two Old Testament verses to amplify the truth that He has just stated at verse 5:17, focusing especially here on the tangible aspect of the "double honor," in terms of remuneration And so, God first quotes from Deuteronomy 25:4, when He says here, "You shall not muzzle the ox while he is threshing," which literally meant that the ox should be allowed to eat of the grain that it was being used to thresh without being muzzled, on the threshing floor after the harvest, which muzzle would be preventing it from eating if it was put on.

Then God goes on to quote from what His Son said, as recorded at Matthew 10:10 and Luke 10:7, which would have come from what was said at Deuteronomy 24:15, namely, "The laborer is worthy of his wages," in that each person deserves to be paid for work done. And here God uses these two quotes to amplify the truth that elders also should be remunerated for the work that they do, in that their support should come from the believers of the congregation that they are part of and on whose behalf they labor!

Then God goes on to give Timothy a second instruction at verses 5:19, 20 and says that an accusation against an elder should not be entertained except on the basis of two or three witnesses making that same accusation. This also is a principle that God quotes from the Old Testament, this time from Deuteronomy 19:15, where God stated, "A single witness shall not rise up against a man on account of any iniquity or any sin which he has committed; on the evidence of two or three witnesses a matter shall be confirmed." If there is only one witness, then it is simply one person's word against the word of the accused, which cannot confirm a matter. However, if there are two or more witnesses saying the same thing, then that testimony is harder for one to refute and should suffice to conclude a matter. In this way, God is simply ensuring that one is not unfairly accused by every person that might have a grudge or a dislike for a person, while at the same time bringing a true judgment when that is warranted.

If two or three witnesses do come forward and make an accusation against an elder, then that needs to be taken seriously, in that the accusation, which as we see here would involve some sin committed by an elder, must be dealt with, which should be handled in private, if this is a first occurrence. However, as God goes on to point out at verse 20, if an elder goes on in the sin that he had previously been accused of and been confronted on in private, then at that point that elder should be rebuked in front of all the believers of that local church when gathered together, which will serve as a warning to other elders of what happens when a leader, who is there to be an example to the flock (noting 1 Peter 5:2,3), sins so as to bring shame and disrepute to that local church.

God's Son gave His disciples the same principles being applied here, when He said to them at Matthew 18:15-17, "[15] If your brother sins, go and show him his fault in private; if he listens to you, you have won your brother. [16] But if he does not listen to you, take one or two more with you, so that by the mouth of two or three witnesses every fact may be confirmed. [17] If he refuses to listen to them, tell it to the church; and if he refuses to listen even to the church, let him be to you as a Gentile and a tax collector." The only exceptions here at verses 5:19,20 are that this is now applied to elders and God does not directly say that the elder who sinned is to be regarded as an unbeliever, although the fourth instruction that God gives at verse 5:22 will touch on this last point, as we will see.

Then God's third instruction to Timothy is at verse 5:23, where God tells him that he is to carry out the first two instructions without bias, that is, without any favoritism on his part for one person against another. God is aware what human nature is like, that we are all indwelt of a sinful nature that always wants to go astray, and that there is a devil in the world who always seeks to draw us astray from what is the right thing to do. This is why God here also says to Timothy through the apostle Paul that he is being given this instruction as a solemn charge in the hearing of God and of His Son, The Lord Jesus Christ, and even of the unfallen angels, because these are matters that are to taken very seriously by all, simply because this is a matter that God Himself takes very seriously!

For God knows that if an elder was to be treated differently than another elder in the matter of remuneration that one deserves, or dealt with differently if one sins, that such bias would no doubt be a cause for eventual division in the local church, which would only serve the devil's purpose! So God wants every believer to be treated alike, not only because God Himself never shows any partiality to anyone (noting Acts 10:34 and Romans 2:11), but also because He is always watching what is taking place in HIS CHURCH on earth!

God's fourth and final instruction to Timothy regarding the elders is at verse 5:22, where God now tells him to "not lay hands upon anyone too hastily and thereby share responsibility for the sins of others; keep yourself free from sin." What God has in view here is when a man is being appointed an elder and all the other elders place their hands on him, as we have seen done at Acts 13:3, when Barnabas and Saul were appointed as apostles by God, and then also earlier at verse 4:14, when Timothy himself was gifted by God as an evangelist. Again, the laying of hands simply indicated that one was in agreement with what God was in the process of doing, and that one agreed to support that person thereafter in whatever way would be needed.

It is important to grasp here that one reason God gives this instruction is to make Timothy (and us) realize that the appointment of a man as an elder is a serious matter, which one should not ever rush into, which means that one is to be certain that God is calling and gifting a man for ministry before one agrees to lay one's hands with the others, for as we saw in the second instruction, if that elder is later found to be one who continues in sin, even after being confronted in private, and then rebuked in the presence of the congregation, then that makes those who partook in the laying of hands look bad, as if to say that the man should never have been appointed as an elder in the first place, for now his appointment is causing more harm than good for the cause of Christ in that place!

1 Timothy 5:23, God's instruction to Timothy regarding his frequent ailments and how to deal with them

What is interesting to see here is that God pauses His instructions to Timothy that he is to apply toward others to now deal with an issue that was frequently affecting Timothy personally, which was his health, saying here to Timothy through the apostle Paul at 1 Timothy 5:23, *"No longer drink water exclusively, but use a little wine for the sake of your stomach and your frequent ailments."*

We have already touched on this verse earlier, when looking at the qualifications for the overseer at verse 3:3, where we said that what was in view here at verse 5:23 was not that God wanted Timothy to start being a wine drinker – for as we see here, it was clear that Timothy did not partake at all, due to God saying, "No longer drink water exclusively – but rather God was instructing Timothy to use a little wine for medicinal purposes, which is not likely what would be said in our day, due to large assortment of knowledge and natural products now available to deal with one's "stomach and frequent ailments." This also shows us here that God sees nothing wrong in using naturally occurring products to maintain one's health!

1 Timothy 5:24,25, two other truths from God that Timothy also needed to be aware of

Because God included verse 5:23 between the previous verses and what He now says at 1 Timothy 5:24,25, this tells us that these are now separate truths that Timothy also needed to be aware of, *"[24] The sins of some men are quite evident, going before them to judgment; for others, their sins follow after. [25] Likewise also, deeds that are good are quite evident, and those which are otherwise cannot be concealed."*

In the first case at verse 5:24 here, God speaks of sins that men commit (speaking of mankind in general here), some "are quite evident," being done in a public way for all to discover, which brings a fairly quick reckoning for those sins, however, "for others, their sins follow after," being sins done in the shadows, which are harder for one to find out about, but which will nevertheless be judged by God one day, who sees all things, even those things done in secret. Let us note here what God tells us at Luke 8:17, "For nothing is hidden that will not become evident, nor anything secret that will not be known and come to light," and also at Hebrews 4:13, "And there is no creature hidden from His sight, but all things are open and laid bare to the eyes of Him with whom we have to do."

Then in God's second truth at verse 5:25, He there indicates that the reverse is also true, now in the case of the good deeds that one does, in that some good deeds are evident for all to see as they are done, while some other deeds are not so evident, but nevertheless will come to light in due time, so that even if humans never find out about them, nevertheless God sees them and He will reward in due time.

And so, the lessons to be learned here are: Do not sin, for it will eventually come to light and you will either face humans in judgment when they come to light, or else God Himself will deal with you directly. And you do not have to worry about being rewarded for good deeds done, for even if you are not in this life, yet God, Who sees all, will Himself reward you in due time. And so, keep on keeping on with God and do not be concerned about your good works, except to ensure that this is what your life is set on carrying on for the glory of God alone!

CHAPTER SIX

1 Timothy 6:1-21

1 Timothy 6:1,2, God's instructions regarding master/slave relationships, which in our day translates into the employer/employee relationships

As God begins this sixth chapter of His first letter to Timothy, He now continues His instructions to Timothy at 1 Timothy 6:1,2, by briefly addressing the master/slave relationship, which in our present day would be in reference to the employer/employee relationship, noting now what God here instructs, *"[1] All who are under the yoke as slaves are to regard their own masters as worthy of all honor so that the name of God and our doctrine will not be spoken against. [2} Those who have believers as their masters must not be disrespectful to them because they are brethren, but must serve them all the more, because those who partake of the benefit are believers and beloved. Teach and preach these principles."*

So what God says to Timothy here at verse 6:1, as instructions that were to be taught to believers, was that "all who are under the yoke," whether that be as believing slaves in those days, or believing employees in ours, that such must regard their master/employer "as worthy of all honor," where these are unbelievers. For if this is not done, in terms of one badmouthing the master/employer, for instance, then one opens the door for the enemy, the devil, to work, which will then result in "the name of God and our doctrine" (that is, the teaching, as part of the local church in that community) will "be spoken against," which would be by the unbelieving master/employer, and would obviously be of no benefit to anyone, except the devil.

Then God goes on and says at verse 6:2 that if a believing slave or employee has a master/employer who is a fellow believer, then one "must not be disrespectful to them because they are brethren, but must serve them all the more, because those who partake of the benefit are believers and beloved." For what we need to grasp in the present instance here is that now both groups would be believers in the same community, which also mean that they would be part of the same local church. And if one, as a slave/employee, does not render service to the master/employer, that is in a manner that reflects one's profession of faith in God, then one is in effect again opening the door for the devil to work, not only in one's personal relationship with the master/employer, but also extend to the local church itself, where both would be attending. So God is simply providing commonsense instructions here that are designed for good human relations, which will not give the devil any foothold in which to work division and evil!

1 Timothy 6:3-10, God calls Timothy to adhere to the doctrine of godliness, as it has been taught to him

As God continues, He now calls Timothy, at 1 Timothy 6:3-10, to ensure that he is adhering to the doctrine of godliness in his ministry, noting to begin with what God says at 1 Timothy 6:3-6, "[3] *If anyone advocates a different doctrine and does not agree with sound words, those of our Lord Jesus Christ, and with the doctrine conforming to godliness, [4] he is* conceited and understands nothing; but he has a morbid interest in controversial questions and disputes about words, out of which arise envy, strife, abusive language, evil suspicions, [5] and constant friction between men of depraved mind and deprived of the truth, who suppose that godliness is a means of gain. *[6] But godliness actually is a means of great gain when accompanied by contentment.*"

When God begins at verse 6:3 here and says, "If anyone advocates a different doctrine," He is making reference to the doctrine, that is, the teaching, relating to godliness, which God already made known at verse 3:16, where we saw that God's Son, The Lord Jesus Christ, was the perfect embodiment of that Godliness, when He was here on earth in human likeness at His first coming from Heaven, in that He lived a holy life for the purpose of accomplishing His Father's will while here, as what brought pleasure to His Father's heart.

Then we further saw from verses 4:6,7 that Timothy was himself well on his way of living a life of godliness, as he was there said to be constantly nourishing himself on the words of the faith and its sound teaching, as found in God's word. We there further noted that a life of godliness is being lived when one is living by God's imparted righteous life (that is, His righteousness) moment by moment, with no known unconfessed sins in one's life.

It is also clear that God has the doctrine of godliness in view here, based on what He goes on to say in the rest of verse 6:3, "with the doctrine conforming to godliness," which is not only a teaching that "The Lord Jesus Christ" Himself adhered to and taught, but is a teaching that is in accordance "with sound words," relating here to all that is contained in God's word, the Bible.

God goes on at verse 6:4,5 and says that if anyone does not adhere to the doctrine of godliness, in terms of either not practicing it, or of advocating a different doctrine, then we can be sure that such a person is "conceited and understands nothing; but he has a morbid interest in controversial questions and disputes about words, out of which arise envy, strife, abusive language, evil suspicions, [5] and constant friction between men of depraved mind and deprived of the truth, who suppose that godliness is a means of gain." In other words, one will either adhere to the doctrine of godliness, for which God's Son left us the Pattern for in Himself while on earth at His first coming, or else one will live a life on earth that is evil, which pleases only the devil and his minions, which is the life that characterizes those who are yet unbelievers, who do not know God or His truth, who only see godliness as just another means of benefiting and enriching themselves!

As God goes on and says at verse 6:6, godliness definitely is a "means of great gain when accompanied by contentment." In other others, when one adheres to a life of godliness and is content with that, not seeking something else on top of that, as if a life of godliness was not enough of itself. The reality to be grasped here is that all those believers, who have truly experienced the life of godliness, in terms of living only by God's imparted righteous life, with no known unconfessed sins in one's life, such have found that life to be more than abundant to satisfy one's being while on earth!

As God goes on and now points out from 1 Timothy 6:7-10, man's attempts at living a material life on earth, instead of a life of godliness, have only "wandered away from the faith and pierced themselves with many griefs," as we now see, *"[7] For we have brought nothing into the world, so we cannot take anything out of it either. [8] If we have food and covering, with these we shall be content. [9] But those who want to get rich fall into temptation and a snare and many foolish and harmful desires which plunge men into ruin and destruction. [10] For the love of money is a root of all sorts of evil, and some by longing for it have wandered away from the faith and pierced themselves with many griefs."*

What God points out here at verse 6:7 is that when we entered this world at physical birth, we had nothing but our birthday suit on, and we can be sure that in the same way, when we leave this life, which for most will be at physical death, we will definitely not be bringing anything of a material nature along with us! For what needs to be grasped here is that the afterlife that all experience after this life, whether as a believer or an unbeliever, is a spiritual life, and not material at all. This means that as human beings our focus while on earth should not be on material things and their accumulation, but rather we should be concerned with obtaining eternal life with God and then adhering to a life of godliness for one's remaining days on earth!

As God goes on to point out at verse 6:8, if we have food and clothes with which to cover ourselves, we should be content with that! Some might be surprised to hear God say "food and covering" here, which refers to the very basics for existence on earth! In other words, God does not oppose human beings, even believers, having a house to live in, a car to drive, and some money in the bank, as we see in Scripture that many believers, such as Abraham, David, and Solomon, for examples, were made rich by God Himself while on earth, although what God gives is always for the purpose of putting it to use in His service! The point is, however, that the contentment that God wants us to have as believers while yet on earth, of what is material in nature, is for us all to be satisfied with food and clothing, while adhering to a life of godliness, with whatever else God may add being added only for the purpose of serving Him!

That is why God goes on and points out what He does at verse 6:9, namely that "those who want to get rich fall into temptation and a snare and many foolish and harmful desires which plunge men into ruin and destruction." What God is pointing out here is also what He pointed out at verses 6:4,5, namely that those who seek a life other than a life of godliness while on earth are seeking what is not of God, but is of the devil, who always either opposes or counterfeits what is of God. What this means then, relating to what God said at verse 6:8, in terms of warning us as humans to be satisfied with the basics of this life, which are food and clothing, for the simple reason that those who seek more than this on their own apart from God, are only giving the devil an opening to work in their lives, for he will then tempt with all kinds of desires and temptations that are not of God, with the end result being to plunge one into ruin and destruction, with the word "destruction" here not speaking of no longer existing, but rather of loss of spiritual wellbeing, if one had it to begin with!

What God then goes on to point out at verse 6:10 is that those of verse 6:9 who "want to get rich" do so simply because they have "the love of money," which God says is "a root of all sorts of evil," where we are to see that the word "sorts" is an added word, so that the literal rendering here is "a root of all the evils." In other words, since the dawn of time, men and women have been known to commit any crime (sin) for money! A famous line in many movies is, "Name your price," which means that everyone who is not living a life of godliness on earth has a price; that is, one only needs to come to the amount of money that one will yield to temptation for, and the person will commit the evil in question, whether that be murder, adultery, fornication, robbing a bank, etc.

We need to take what God says here very seriously, especially if one is a Christian, and especially if one is a Christian and living in the materially rich Western Hemisphere, for as God goes on to point out in the rest of verse 6:10 here, "some by longing for it (that is for the riches that money can buy) have wandered away from the faith and pierced themselves with many griefs." The most miserable people in the world are not the poor, but rather the rich, for the love of money is an opium that only causes one to want more, which one will then be willing to do anything to achieve, which can only result in one being poorer and poorer in the things that really matter in life, starting with a right relationship with God, which is at the root of true happiness!

God begins at 1 Timothy 6:11 by telling Timothy to flee from the things that are not of God, in order to pursue the things that are, namely a godly life, as we now see, *"But flee from these things, you man of God, and pursue righteousness, godliness, faith, love, perseverance and gentleness."* In other words, Timothy was to flee from a godless life as we have just seen God describe, to instead live a life that is godly, which consists of living by God's imparted righteous life (His righteousness); of living a holy life for the will of God, as His Son did while on earth, which is what pleases God; of living by faith and not be sight, continually trusting God in all things and no matter what happens; of living a life of love, which is characterized by a total self-giving, first to God and then in service to others; in living a life of patient enduring, of keeping on going on, even when things are tough and the road is rough; and living a humble life in a submissive and non-combatant frame of mind and disposition.

We are also to note here that God calls Timothy a, "man of God" at verse 6:11, which is a term used throughout Scripture for a man called into God's service in order to live a life dedicated to the service of God. And so for instance, we see the term first applied to Moses in The Old Testament, such as at Deuteronomy 33:1 and to a prophet, noting 1 Samuel 9:6-14; while in the New Testament, we only have the term used here at 1 Timothy 6:11, and then also at 2 Timothy 3:17, where we read, adding verse 16 for context, "[16] All Scripture is inspired by God and profitable for teaching, for reproof, for correction, for training in righteousness; [17] so that the man of God may be adequate, equipped for every good work."

God continues at 1 Timothy 6:12 and now tells Timothy that he must not only live a godly life, but that he must also do two things, which are to: *"Fight the good fight of faith; take hold of the eternal life to which you were called, and you made the good confession in the presence of many witnesses."* So the first thing that God wants Timothy to do here in fighting the good fight of the faith is to contend for the faith, which would be by continuously and earnestly battling all opposition and temptations. At verse 1:18 earlier, we there saw that God called Timothy to also "fight the good fight," where the two words "fight" were two different Greek words than are used here by God at verse 6:12. There at verse 1:18, God was calling Timothy to engage in the spiritual warfare that comes from not only being a child of God yet in the world, but also as a servant of God as a minister of the gospel as an evangelist.

Then the second thing God calls Timothy to at 6:12 is to "take hold of the eternal life to which you were called…" In other words, he was to take a hold of the eternal life, which he received from God as a free gift at the moment of his salvation, in the sense that he was to appropriate for himself all the benefits, privileges, and responsibilities associated with the reception of that eternal life from God! When God goes on to add at the end of verse 6:12, "and you made the good confession in the presence of many witnesses," God is here making reference either to when Timothy received water baptism shortly after his salvation, or when he was called of God into fulltime ministry as an evangelist, as we have seen at verse 4:14. It is common to see a testimony of one's salvation at both those occasions.

However, based on what follows at verse 6:13 here, it is more likely that "the good confession" that Timothy made in the presence of many witnesses was when He was called of God into the ministry as an evangelist. It should also be mentioned here that there is no such thing in Scripture as the 'ordination' of a minister of God. Such men simply have a direct calling of God to the ministry, which is then acknowledged by those who are the elders of the local church where one is attending, which elders then lay hands on that man to indicate that they agree with the call of God, due to God having made it known to them also, and they then lay hands on the man being called of God in order to show support for that man, in terms of prayer and tangible support.

Then as we see at 1 Timothy 6:13-16, God gives Timothy a charge through the apostle Paul, when He says to him, *"[13] I charge you in the presence of God, who gives life to all things, and of Christ Jesus, who testified the good confession before Pontius Pilate, [14] that you keep the commandment without stain or reproach until the appearing of our Lord Jesus Christ, [15] which He will bring about at the proper time — He who is the blessed and only Sovereign, the King of kings and Lord of lords, [16] who alone possesses immortality and dwells in unapproachable light, whom no man has seen or can see. To Him be honor and eternal dominion! Amen."*

God's charge to Timothy here is as we see at verses 6:13,14, when God says to him, "I charge you… that you keep the commandment without stain or reproach…" God used that same Greek word here rendered "charge" at verse 1:3, where it was rendered 'instruct,' which will also be rendered as such again at verse 6:17 later in this chapter. Then we are to also see that the Greek word rendered here as "charge" at verse 6:13 was earlier rendered as 'prescribe' at both verses 4:11 and 5:7. And so, God's charge to Timothy here at 6:13,14 is for him to "keep the commandment without stain or reproach," meaning that Timothy was to watch over, guard, all the teachings of God's word with which he had been entrusted, in order to then pass on to others as part of his ministry, doing so without alteration in the message he proclaims, and without anyone being able to accuse him of any wrongdoing in the discharge of his ministry as an evangelist!

We also see from verses 6:13 that God adds that this charge to Timothy through the apostle Paul was being made to him, "in the presence of God," Who not only "gives life to all things," in that He preserves alive all things that has the breath of life in it; but Who, as we have seen already, sees all things that are done on earth, so that He can withdraw that breath at any time from any living thing, so that it will cease to exist on earth!

As we then further see from verse 6:13, this charge was also being made in the presence "of Christ Jesus," Who Himself while on earth, "testified the good confession before Pontius Pilate," which is in reference to after God's Son had been arrested by the leadership of the nation of Israel yet in unbelief, and after He had then been turned over to the Romans, being then judged at Jerusalem by Pontius Pilate, the Roman governor over the province of Judea. We see this confession in the gospel accounts of Matthew, Mark, Luke, and John, for each time God's Son was asked a question, He gave an answer that was appropriate not only with the question, but also in line with God's word and the will of God for His life at that moment!

Then we see from verses 6:14,15 that Timothy was to guard and watch over all the teachings of God's word "until the appearing of our Lord Jesus Christ, which He (God The Father) will bring about at the proper time," which is in reference to the end of the present third age of time, when God's Son returns at the first stage of His second coming, which is when all the believers of the present age will be removed from the earth, along with The Holy Spirit, as we see for instance at 1 Thessalonians 4:14-17 with 2 Thessalonians 2:7.

The "He" at verse 6:15, Who will bring this about at the proper time, is none else but God The Father, Who then leads the apostle Paul to write at verses 6:15,16, "[15] …He who is the blessed and only Sovereign, the King of kings and Lord of lords, [16] who alone possesses immortality and dwells in unapproachable light, whom no man has seen or can see. To Him be honor and eternal dominion! Amen."

When God The Father is referred to as "He who is the blessed and only Sovereign," this is a reference to the fact that it is from God The Father that the highest good originates, by which mankind on earth is blessed, and also the only One, Who is over all things and Who controls all things, so that nothing ever occurs from the time of the original creation until eternity future without God's involvement in its occurrence, so that all that occurs is only in order to fulfill His eternal plan that He placed in motion for the four ages of time, noting for instance what we read at 1 Corinthians 8:6 in part, "…there is but one God, the Father, from whom are all things…," and also at Ephesians 1:11 in part, "…according to His purpose who works all things after the counsel of His will…"

God The Father is also seen here at verse 6:15 as being "the King of kings and Lord of lords," in that He is The King, Who, through His Son, The Lord Jesus Christ, is above all human kings on earth, and also Lord above all human lords on earth! And then at verse 6:16, we see that God The Father "alone possesses immortality," in the sense that He cannot ever die, since death was a consequence of sin (noting Genesis 2:16,17) and God is ever sinless, and also in the sense that death is part of what it means to be mortal, that is, a human being, which God The Father never is, being always a spirit Being, noting John 4:24.

It is true that God's Son, The Lord Jesus Christ, did die a physical death at the cross, which was possible only after He had taken on the sinless human body that His Father had prepared for Him in the womb of the virgin (noting Hebrews 10:5 with Matthew 1:18-25), and then went to the cross, where He died a death He did not deserve to die, but which was necessary in order to pay the penalty due the sins of the whole of the human race, before being buried and then raised from the dead the third day, so that He would provide His Father a basis for the forgiveness of sins and the granting of eternal life to all those who would believe in Him for salvation.

We are then further told at verse 6:16 that God The Father, "dwells in unapproachable light," in that He exists in light that no human being can ever approach. The reason for this can be determined from what we are told at 1 John 1:5, "This is the message we have heard from Him and announce to you, that God is Light (same word), and in Him there is no darkness at all." What this means then is that no human being can ever approach God, because all human beings have been tainted with the original sin of Adam and Eve in the soul.

Only God's Son (noting John 1:18; Colossians 1:15; Hebrews 1:2,3) and the unfallen angels (noting Luke 1:19; Hebrews 12:22) can approach God The Father and dwell in His Presence in that unapproachable light. Only after human beings have been glorified, that is, only after one has been brought to Heaven in the first resurrection, when one's sinful nature is removed from the soul and one's physical body is rendered a spiritual body (noting 1 Corinthians 15:42-44) will human beings enter God's Presence in Heaven, which of course is reserved only for believers of the four ages of time.

Then God concludes His self-disclosure at verse 6:16 by telling Timothy through the apostle Paul that He is "whom no man has seen or can see," simply because He lives in that unapproachable light in which no human beings can approach, which is why God The Father has revealed Himself for both time and eternity as always dwelling in, speaking from, and working through His Son, The Lord Jesus Christ! Even when we, as human believers, are in God's Presence after our time of glorification in the first resurrection, we will still only ever see God The Father by looking at His Son, which will be so for all eternity to come, noting John 14:7-10 and Revelation 21:1-4.

And because of these great truths, that is why, we then read at the end of verse 6:16, "To Him (God The Father, through His Son by The Holy Spirit) be honor and eternal dominion! Amen," that is, The One Who is held in high valuation, for Whom one holds a high estimation due to His manifested all-power over all creation! He, God The

Father alone is worthy indeed of all honor and dominion. Amen, amen, and amen!

1 Timothy 6:17-19, God's instructions to Timothy regarding those believers who had been blessed with the riches of this world

As we now see from 1 Timothy 6:17-19, God now gives Timothy instructions to pass on to those believers he would be in contact with, who had been blessed with the riches of this present life, noting now what God tells him, *"[17] Instruct those who are rich in this present world not to be conceited or to fix their hope on the uncertainty of riches, but on God, who richly supplies us with all things to enjoy. [18] Instruct them to do good, to be rich in good works, to be generous and ready to share, [19] storing up for themselves the treasure of a good foundation for the future, so that they may take hold of that which is life indeed."*

What God wants Timothy to tell those believers he came in contact with, "who are rich in this present world," as we see to begin with at verse 6:17, is that "they are not to be conceited," that is, they are not to be so high-minded as to think that their wealth was due to what they had done apart from God, which would then lead them to think they were above others due to having that wealth! Such thinking as this was not only dishonoring to God, but was also a sin!

Instead, God calls rich believers "to fix their hope… on God," due to "the uncertainty of riches." These well-to-do believers were to realize that they had these riches only because of God, and only given to serve God's purposes, which meant that God could remove those riches at any time, if one were not using the riches to serve God, and instead one used them for one's own pleasures! God does provide all things for us to enjoy as believers, as God goes on to disclose here, but only in the will of God for our lives, not outside His will, for this would then be akin to a man being hired and being paid by one firm, but all his time is spent laboring for another firm.

Then God goes on at verse 6:18 and discloses to Timothy why God gave wealth to certain believers, which was that they might use that wealth "to do good," so as to then be found "to be rich in good works," because now they are using that wealth as God intended it to be used, for the accomplishing of God's purposes and for His glory, and not for one's own pleasure. When a believer is in the will of God, then one will use one's riches to help the less fortunate as God leads one to do so.

This last point is an important one here, in that all that we do must be in the will of God, or else it is a sin. It is as much a sin to help the less fortunate when God does not lead us to do so, as it is a sin not to share our bounty with others as God directs us to do so! We have to be sensitive to God in all our dealings with others, for at times God may be withholding help from a believer due to that believer being outside the will of God. And if one helps such a believer, then one is marring God's attempt to teach that believer to depend on Him and to walk with Him!

God ends His instruction to rich believers at verse 6:19 by pointing out that when they use their God-given wealth in the will of God, meaning as He directs one to do, then one is not only always being "generous and ready to share" with the less fortunate that God is directing one to help, but one is also "storing up for themselves the treasure of a good foundation for the future," speaking here of not only to being rewarded of God in the afterlife, but also benefiting now while still on earth, because they will have taken "hold of that which is life indeed," in terms of having learned to walk with God at the center of His will, which starts by one having learned to live only by God's own imparted life (that is, His righteousness) with no known unconfessed sins in one's life!

Let us note from Matthew 6:20,21 what God's Son taught His followers while one earth at His first coming, "[20] But store up for yourselves treasures in heaven, where neither moth nor rust destroys, and where thieves do not break in or steal; [21] for where your treasure is, there your heart will be also." So just as what comes out of one's mouth reveals our hearts before God, as to whether we are walking with Him or not; so too in the use of riches that God supplies us, in that the way we use those riches reveals our hearts to God and to a watching world. What God is looking for from us as believers is for a walk and a talk that is in line with God's will, so that we might honor and glorify God while on earth, just as His Son did while He was on earth, noting John 17:4! Only then will we have taken hold of the abundant life that God's Son came to earth to give us, noting John 10:10!

As we then see from 1 Timothy 6:20,21, God brings His first letter to Timothy to a close by giving him some final instructions through the apostle Paul, *"[20] O Timothy, guard what has been entrusted to you, avoiding worldly and empty chatter and the opposing arguments of what is falsely called "knowledge"— [21] which some have professed and thus gone astray from the faith. Grace be with you."* As we see here, God is aware that it is easy for us as believers to be led astray from the faith, which is one reason why God at times uses the imagery of a shepherd with his sheep, in speaking of His Son with believers, noting for instance Psalm 23; Isaiah 53:6; and John 10. And so, God knows that as an evangelist, Timothy must himself be strong in the faith and not be lead astray from it, if he is to reach others for God, in terms to sharing the gospel with them. God knows that the devil likes to strike the shepherd so that the flock might be scattered, noting Matthew 26:31.

So that is why God concludes His instructions to Timothy here by telling him to make sure he guards well the truth that he has been entrusted with since coming to know God, as all that God has taught him, either directly through the word of God, or through other believers such as the apostle Paul, who were more advanced in the faith in God they shared. God mentions two things here, which He knows the devil likes to get believers involved with in order to lead them away from the faith, these being "worldly and empty chatter" and "the opposing arguments of what is falsely called "knowledge.""

When God speaks of "empty chatter" here, He is making reference to getting caught up in discussions that are not of God, and therefore lead nowhere and accomplish nothing of lasting value, which is why He terms these "worldly" here, and which are only designed of the evil one to lead one astray, who is a believer. We see a good example of this at Genesis 3:1-5, where we see the devil come to Eve in the guise of a serpent and starts a conversation with her, which was outside of God's will and was only designed to lead her astray from God. This is why God says at 2 Corinthians 11:3, "But I am afraid that, as the serpent deceived Eve by his craftiness, your minds will be led astray from the simplicity and purity of devotion to Christ." God also repeats the same instruction in his second letter to

Timothy, at 2 Timothy 2:16, and there tells him why he was to avoid worldly and empty chatter, because "it will lead to further ungodliness."

Then the "knowledge" that God instructs Timothy to be on guard against is knowledge that did not have its source in God, which is why God refers to this as "what is falsely called "knowledge"" here, which would be spread about by those having "opposing arguments," that is, by people having an opposing view contrary to what is of God. It is important to keep in mind here that there are only two sources of knowledge in the world, God and the devil. What is of God is called truth and is good for one's wellbeing on earth, while the other is of the devil, is a lie and evil, only designed to lead mankind away from the truth of God! And that is exactly what the devil was successful in doing with Eve in the garden of Eden at Genesis 3:1-5!

As we see at verse 6:21, God is very much aware that empty worldly chatter and false knowledge are two of the tools used by the devil that some believers had already been led away from the faith by, although not meaning that they had lost their salvation, which it is impossible for a one born spiritually into God's family by means of the indwelling Holy Spirit to do, but rather meaning that one has been led astray from walking with God, so that as long as one is in that state, one is not useful to God in His service, in terms of carrying out His will on earth as a child of His.

And since God did not want this to happen to Timothy, He leads the apostle to close His letter to Timothy with the words, "Grace be with you." In other words, 'may God's unmerited favor continue to work in your life without interruption,' as it did in the life of the apostle Paul, who was led of God to write at 1 Corinthians 15:10, "But by the grace of God I am what I am, and His grace toward me did not prove vain; but I labored even more than all of them, yet not I, but the grace of God with me."

To God alone be all praise, honor, and glory, with thanksgiving, both now and forevermore! Amen, amen, and amen.

ADDENDUM A

/ The four ages of time

What is important to know when reading God's word, the Bible, is that God has divided time into four ages. And since God's word covers all of time, then all of God's word, the Bible, can be subdivided along the lines of these four ages. But before noting what these four ages are, we need to also be aware that in each of the four ages of time, God uses the believers of that age as His vessels. In other words, God is accomplishing His work on earth through the believers of each age of time.

And what is also important to keep in mind in regards to this is that although God starts each age with believers, before long the number of unbelievers in each age outnumbers the number of believers. In other words, one characteristic of each age of time is that there is a believing remnant among a mass of unbelievers, with these believers in each age being those whom God preserves for Himself and through whom God works to accomplish His purposes in each age through time.

And so, in the first age of time God worked through Adam and his believing descendants as His vessels to accomplish His will on earth, which age covers the first eleven chapters of Genesis. What this means is that they were the believers who willingly served Him out of love for Him. In other words, this was the believing line of descent, or the believing remnant, through which God worked out His will.

Then when we begin Genesis 12, we see God take one believer, Abraham, and out of that one man's descendants through the line of Isaac, and then through the line of Jacob, God makes a nation, which is Israel. And again, we need to see that only the believing line of descent within the nation of Israel was the remnant through which God worked to accomplish His will. What this means is that not all those who were of the nation of Israel were believers. In fact, the majority were unbelievers. Therefore, in the second age of time, which goes from Genesis 12 to the end of Malachi in the Old Testament, and includes the gospel accounts of Matthew, Mark, Luke, and John, plus Acts 1 and Revelation 6 to 19 in the New Testament, God works out His will in time through the believers of the nation of Israel, which is again a small number compared to the total number.

And here we need to pause for a moment and mention something else before going on to consider the third age of time, and this is the fact of representation. What this means is that in the first age of time, we have Adam and Eve as our first parents, who were but representative of all people on earth. In other words, God knew that what this one couple did, any other couple would have done the same thing, since God knows that once sin entered His perfect and sinless creation, we all would have the same sinful nature as human beings.

Then the same is true in regards to the nation of Israel in the second age of time, in that God knew that what this one nation did, any other nation on earth would likewise have done had it been chosen by God as a representative nation. So when God set out to make the one nation of Israel, He started out with just believers. But when the nation of Israel came into existence later, only a believing remnant within the nation were believers. Now since the nation of Israel was but representative of all the nations, then God knew that if He had chosen any other nation on earth, He would find that only a believing remnant would ever become believers to serve Him willingly out of love for Him out of a mass of unbelievers, who would not in any of those nations. In other words, no other human being would have acted any differently than our first parents, and likewise, no other nation would have acted any differently than the nation of Israel did. This means that all human beings and all nations are likewise guilty before God!

What also needs to be mentioned here as we now go on to look at the third age of time, is that the first two ages basically relate to the time period covered by the Old Testament, which means that the third and fourth ages of time must be covered by the New Testament portion of God's word, the Bible. And let us recall that in the first age, God worked through the believers of that age, beginning with Adam, while in the second age of time, God works through the believers of the nation of Israel, beginning with Abraham. So as we come to the third age of time, which goes from Acts 2 to the end of Revelation 5 in God's word, the Bible, we have God working through the believers of earth, whom God calls "the church."

What this means then is that in this third age of time, which we are presently still in, God is accomplishing His will through all the believers of earth, with God now not looking at any specific nation in particular. In other words, during the present third age of time, also known as 'the church age,' the nation of Israel, although being supernaturally preserved by God, is still just the same as any other nation on earth, having a believing remnant among a majority of unbelievers.

Then in the fourth age of time, which is basically covered by Revelation 20 to 22 in the New Testament, although mentioned often in prophecy in various portions of the Old Testament, we have God working through the believers of that age, but now with much greater variation. In other words, during the fourth age of time God works through the believers of every nation on earth still in their natural bodies, and also through the believers of the first three ages of time, who would have experienced their part in the first resurrection relating to believers and who are now in their resurrected bodies! This is covered in much greater detail in my book, "An Introduction To The New World That Is Coming Upon The Earth," which focuses on this fourth age of time. If there are any readers who are not sure of what is meant by the first and second resurrection and the fact of people serving God in their new resurrected bodies in the future, please see my book, "Have You Ever Wondered What Happens After Death?"

Before leaving this Addendum, it is also important to be aware that the Old Testament portion of God's word, the Bible, contains 39 books, which deal with the beginning of all things in God's plan of the ages, while the New Testament portion of God's word, the Bible, contains 27 books, which deal with the consummation of all things in

God's eternal plan, which God is outworking through the four ages of time.

Also of great value is to know that the second age of time is not completed until AFTER the completion of the present third age of time. In other words, there are seven years remaining in the second age of time dealing with the nation of Israel, which is why this nation is being supernaturally preserved by God during this present third age, simply because God is not yet finished outworking His plan of the ages through that nation. These seven years remaining is a time of God's judgment against all unbelievers of earth and is approximately covered by Revelation 6:1 to Revelation 19:21 in God's word, although also mentioned often in prophecy in the Bible.

What also needs to be mentioned and is important to remember is that the reason God has a series of ages in time is in order to show us just how sinful the human race is and just how incapable it is of doing good, in terms of pleasing God on its own apart from God. What is meant here is that God's revelation of Himself increases as time progresses, so that those living in the fourth age of time as compared to the first age of time will have a far greater knowledge of God. In other words, as each age progresses, God makes it easier and easier for human beings on earth to come to know Him and to serve Him out of love for Him. For example, in the first two ages, God's precious Son had not yet come to earth, so that He was represented only through types, such as the animal sacrifices and offerings, and in prophecy. Human beings at that time also only had the Old Testament as light to guide them.

But by the time we reach the fourth age of time, God's precious Son will not only have come from Heaven to earth bodily, but will actually be on earth reigning over the nations as King. Please note what God says at Isaiah 11:9 in part, as just one example, "…For the earth will be full of the knowledge of the Lord as the waters cover the sea." What this means then is that when God's final judgment of time comes, relating to all the unbelievers of time (noting Revelations 20:11-15), then none of these unbelievers of time will be able to stand before God and give any excuse for their sin of unbelief, in having personally and freely rejected God's offer of salvation found in His own precious Son, The Lord Jesus Christ. And so, each succeeding age adds to mankind's culpability before a Holy and altogether Righteous God, so that in the end "every mouth may be closed and all the world may become accountable to God" (noting Romans 3:19 in part).

ADDENDUM B

/ The two comings from Heaven to earth of God's precious Son, our Lord Jesus Christ

Another very important truth to know here is that God's word, the Bible, mentions two comings of God's precious Son, The Lord Jesus Christ, from Heaven to earth. His first coming from Heaven to earth was for the purpose of taking on a body like ours, only in the innocence of Adam and as born of a virgin so as not to incur our sinful nature, and then after living thirty-three and half years on earth carrying out only the will of God His Father in absolute sinlessness out of love for Him, was given over into the hands of unbelievers to be put to death on a cross, before being buried, then resurrected from the dead the third day. And of course, His death was not due to anything God's precious Son, The Lord Jesus Christ, had ever done wrong, but rather was to pay the penalty due our sins, which was death, in order that God might have a basis by which to forgive the sins of those who believe in Him.

Then the second coming of God's precious Son is to be seen as being in two stages. The first stage of His second coming is at the end of this present third age of time, and is for the purpose of bringing to Heaven all believers of earth before God's judgment falls on the unbelievers of the earth, thereby bringing the present third age to a close. God has this first stage in view especially at 1 Thessalonians 4:14-17, although also mentioned in many portions of the New Testament.

Then the second stage of the second coming of God's precious Son, The Lord Jesus Christ, occurs at the end of the seven years of God's judgment, which will end the second age of time. God's precious Son would now be coming for one last battle against God's foes, as led by the devil, before establishing His reign on earth as King during the fourth age of time. This is again disclosed by God in many portions of God's word in the New Testament, but especially in passages such as Matthew 24 and Revelation 19:11-21.

ADDENDUM C

/ The relation of apostles and prophets in the early church, and of evangelists and shepherd/teachers in the later church, to the elders in the local church

What would be helpful here is to see the establishment and functioning of a local church as intended by God from the start of the church age at Acts 2:1-4 until that church ends with the removal of all believers from the earth at the first stage of the second coming of God's precious Son, The Lord Jesus Christ, from Heaven to earth. And so, we will look at this subject while keeping these two divisions of the present church age in view; that is, In looking at the early church under apostles and prophets, from around 33 to 100 AD, which is about the date by which all the letters of the New Testament had been given to man by God. Then we will look at the later church under evangelists and shepherd/teachers, which is from 100 AD to the end of the present church age.

In looking at these two divisions, we will also see the relation between an apostle at first, and an evangelist later, in relation to the elders and the teaching function in the local church. And let us remember that the only ministers God ever has in a local church are as we see at Ephesians 4:11, which are apostles and prophets before the giving of the letters of the New Testament to the church by God, and then evangelists and shepherd/teachers after these letters have all been given.

When we see the church begin at Jerusalem at Acts 2:1-4, with the coming of The Holy Spirit from Heaven to permanently indwell believers on earth, we have the twelve apostles, who had been trained by God's own Son while on earth, now officially begin their public ministry of preaching the gospel. And as the gospel is preached, some believe and become part of the local church at Jerusalem. At this point, we have only the apostles in leadership.

Then at Acts 6:1 to 6, we see men being appointed by the believers of the local church at Jerusalem, which we later learn are deacons, with their function being to assist the apostles, in terms of looking after the temporal affairs of the local church, while the apostles look after the spiritual affairs of the local church, by means of prayer and the ministry of the word.

And that ministry of the word in relation to the believers of the local church is to teach them the word of God, so as to see them rooted and established in the faith. But what needs to be realized here is that at this point, believers only have the Old Testament available to them in written form, with the twelve apostles having knowledge of what God's precious Son, The Lord Jesus Christ, taught them during the three and a half years they walked with Him, being trained by Him to carry on the ministry on earth after He had returned to Heaven again at the ascension. What God's Son taught the twelve apostles while on earth now makes up the germ seeds for what will later form the letters of the New Testament And so, until the letters of the New Testament are given by God, written down, and circulated among the local churches, that and the Old Testament, are all the believers have to go by of the word of God.

If we jump over to Acts 13:1 for a moment, we see another local church having begun at Antioch in Syria, being here told that, "Now there were at Antioch, in the church that was there, prophets and teachers: Barnabas, and Simeon who was called Niger, and Lucius of Cyrene, and Manaen who had been brought up with Herod the tetrarch, and Saul." We are to see here that Barnabas and Saul (later to be referred to as Paul) were the two teachers in view here, while the other three men were the prophets. And we also see here that Barnabas and Paul are here being sent out by God, which sending makes them now apostles, which means they are now preachers of the gospel in public ministry.

Barnabas and Paul then go to various cities where disciples are made, in that people come to a personal relationship with God in believing the gospel. The believers in each of these cities then make up the local church there. Then at Acts 14:23, we see Paul and Barnabas, as apostles, appointing ELDERS in each of the local churches which had been established under their ministry, before they return to the local church at Antioch from which they had gone from.

Now in returning to that local church in Antioch, we have the three men already there in leadership as prophets. They remain there and teach the believers when gathered, with Paul and Barnabas also teaching the believers when gathered, because we have mentioned before that they were teachers, which teaching function they also would have exercised in each of the local churches which God had just established under their ministry, rooting and establishing the believers in each local church until such time as God raised elders. So both apostles and prophets exercised the teaching function in the church gathered, although the apostles were only exercising the teaching function before being sent out by God, but afterwards also being preachers of the gospel, which was primarily to the unsaved.

Now as to the matter of elders, we are to note first of all that to be an elder is to hold an office in a local church, while to be an apostle, prophet, evangelist, or shepherd/teacher is to be a gift given by God to each local church and in the aggregate to the church universal. An apostle at first, as is true of an evangelist now, is not a man gifted by God with the gift of evangelism, as some may think, but rather is himself a gift in his person to the church existing on earth, which is comprised of all believers yet on earth. That an elder holds an office is seen from what God says at 1 Timothy 3:1, where we read, "It is a trustworthy statement: if any man aspires to the office of overseer, it is a fine work he desires to do."

As to the evangelist being a gift from God to His church on earth, we have already noted this from Ephesians 4:7,8,11. Elders are always raised of God from among the believers of a local church, being then recognized as such by the apostle at first, later by the evangelist, as the one having begun that local church through the public preaching of the gospel. One is appointed to the office of elder only after being raised of God. In other words, God is The One Who raises elders, as is clear from what we read at Acts 20:28, where God says to the elders at Ephesus through the apostle Paul, "Be on guard for yourselves and for all the flock, among which the Holy Spirit has made you overseers, to shepherd the church of God which He purchased with His own blood." It is never an apostle or an evangelist who chooses an elder. Rather, they only appoint the men that God has raised, with their being able to identify them through their functioning as such, noting the qualifications they would have based on what God gave at 1 Timothy 3:1-7 and Titus 1:5-9.

And as to the relation between these four gifted men given by God to the church in relation to the elders and the teaching function of the local church, we are to see that before they are gifted by God, which is when their ministry starts, the apostles at first, and then the evangelists, are men holding the office of elders and exercising the teaching function in the local church. In order to see this here, we can now return to the church at Jerusalem, which was the first local church established by God on earth after the church age started at Acts 2. Where we left off above, we had the twelve apostles ministering in that local church, teaching the believers when gathered. Over time, these apostles did the same in this church at Jerusalem as we saw Paul and Barnabas do in the churches they established over the known world, which was to also appoint elders there, from among the believers in that local church. That is why at Acts 15:1-6, we see elders now functioning in that church along with the twelve apostles.

One important truth which we need to be aware of is that although the twelve apostles of God's Son, The Lord Jesus Christ, were the original leaders of the local church at Jerusalem, which had begun through their preaching of the gospel in Jerusalem, nevertheless, they were regarded by God as elders and apostles, even though only recognized as apostles by men. Later, as the believers of that local church at Jerusalem grew spiritually under the teaching ministry of the apostles to establish them in the faith, God raised up elders from among them to carry on the ministry once the apostles were no longer there. That is why we see at Acts 1:20, where God says in regards to finding a replacement for Judas Iscariot, speaking through the apostle Peter says to us what we there read, looking at verses 1:16,17,20 to 26 for context, "[16] "Brethren, the Scripture had to be fulfilled, which the Holy Spirit foretold by the mouth of David concerning Judas, who became a guide to those who arrested Jesus. [17] For he was counted among us and received his share in this ministry... [20] For it is written in the book of Psalms, 'Let his homestead be made desolate, and let no one dwell in it'; and, 'Let another man take his office.' [21] Therefore it is necessary that of the men who have accompanied us all the time that the Lord Jesus went in and out among us — [22] beginning with the baptism of John until the day that He was taken up from us — one of these must become a witness with us of His resurrection." [23] So they put forward two men, Joseph called Barsabbas (who was also called Justus), and Matthias. [24] And they prayed and said, "You, Lord, who know the hearts of all men, show which one of these two You have chosen [25] to occupy this ministry and apostleship from which Judas turned aside to go to his own place." [26] And they drew lots for them, and the lot fell to Matthias; and he was added to the eleven apostles."

We need to note at verse 20 that the word "office" here is the same Greek word as at 1 Timothy 3:1 and literally refers to the same 'office of overseer' that was there in view, which means that Judas Iscariot had this office of an elder as one of the twelve apostles, and which Matthias, as his replacement among the twelve, was now to have, as is clear from verse 25. And so, it was because the apostles were also elders that the apostle Peter refers himself as an elder at 1 Peter 5:1, when addressing believers, "Therefore, I exhort the elders among you, as your fellow elder..." Similarly for the apostle John at 2 John 1:1 and 3 John 1:1. Although the word "elder" has an age component inherent in the word throughout Scripture, and even though the apostle John is no doubt an aged man when led of God to write this, nevertheless, he was not just an apostle, but also an elder in the church.

And coming back full circle to the local church at Antioch in Syria, Paul and Barnabas were elders in that local church before being sent out by God as apostles, where they had been exercising the teaching function, along with the other three elders who were prophets. What this means is that the men who are in the process of being raised of God to be elders in a local church are teachers until such time as raised of God as elders, and then appointed as such by the apostle responsible for establishing that local church.

Then when appointed as an elder, one holds the office of elder, being either gifted by God as an apostle or a prophet. If an elder is gifted as an apostle, then God will send out that elder at some point, which means one has now a call of God and is now sent out by God as an apostle, still holding the office of elder. After all the letters of the New Testament had been given by 100 AD, then elders of local churches throughout the world were either being gifted by God as evangelists or shepherd/teachers, and no longer as apostles and prophets.

Now that we know that the apostles of the early church were replaced by the evangelists, which is to be the case right up to the end of the present church age, we can now quickly summarize what still applies and what does not, relating to what an apostle did then and what an evangelist does now. Evangelist are still sent out by God to preach the gospel in public ministry, having the same two tools available to apostles, that being prayer and the ministry of the word of God. Whereas supernatural sign gifts accompanied the ministry of apostles, yet now for evangelists, all such sign gifts have ceased. Evangelists are also men, who if married are also allowed to take a believing wife along in the public preaching of the gospel

"Jesus said to him, "I am the way, and the truth, and the life; no one comes to the Father but through Me." "

John 14:6

ADDENDUM D

/ For those who may not as yet know God

Possibly you have been reading this book and have become aware of not knowing this God Who created us and gave us physical life into this world, and up to now has allowed you to live on earth. However, you do have the desire to know God in a personal way. If this is the case, then this Addendum has been written specifically for you.

And what God wants you to have in coming to know Him is the peace and joy which comes in knowing that all of your sins committed in your lifetime are forgiven and that you have eternal life with God. And so, your greatest need at the moment is to make peace with God so as to go to Heaven, which is God's eternal home. And so, this Addendum will help to bring that about by pointing you to God so as to come to faith in Him.

And as we begin, we need to note a most important promise which God makes at Romans 6:23 to all those who do not yet know Him, "For the wages of sin is death, but the free gift of God is eternal life in Christ Jesus our Lord." The good news here is that God offers you eternal life with Him as a free gift, which is to be obtained in His Son, Jesus Christ. What God does not do in this verse from the Bible is tell us 'how' to obtain that eternal life with Him.

Another verse which we can look at where God does let us know 'how' one can obtain that eternal life with Him is noting what God tells us at John 3:16, "For God so loved the world, that He gave His only begotten Son, that whoever believes in Him shall not perish, but have eternal life." Now the added truth which God makes known here is that the eternal life, which He gives to a human being as a free gift, is for those who believe in His Son.

Then the question is: What is it that I am to believe about God's Son, Jesus Christ, which will lead God to give me eternal life with Him forever? And the beauty of God is that He never leaves us guessing, especially when it comes to having a personal relationship with Him, which He desires us to have. Therefore, we should not be surprised when God gives us the answer to our question in what He tells us at 1 Corinthians 15:1-4, "[1] Now I make known to you, brethren, the gospel which I preached to you, which also you received, in which also you stand, [2] by which also you are saved, if you hold fast the word which I preached to you, unless you believed in vain. [3] For I delivered to you as of first importance what I also received, that Christ died for our sins according to the Scriptures, [4] and that He was buried, and that He was raised on the third day according to the Scriptures…"

Therefore, "the gospel," which simply means 'good news,' which God wants you to hear and believe in order to "be saved," which simply refers to you coming to know God and have eternal life with Him, is that His Son has already died for you, has already been buried, and has already been raised from the dead again the third day after His death, in order that God would have a basis by which to forgive you of all your sins, which are all against Him, and to freely give you eternal life with Him, for simply believing this message in your heart.

One thing which often prevents a person from believing the gospel at this point is not seeing oneself as a sinner before a Holy God. When we look at ourselves by our own assessment, and especially when we compare ourselves with others around us, we often think of ourselves as being better than others, and so good enough to enter Heaven in our present condition. The problem with this is that it is the product of our own thinking and is not God's assessment of our situation.

God's assessment of our situation is as He tells us at Romans 3:10-12,23 in part, "[10] as it is written, "There is none righteous, not even one… [11] there is none who seeks for God [12] all have turned aside… there is none who does good, there is not even one... [23] for all have sinned and fall short of the glory of God…" Quite a different assessment of the human race from that which we as human beings often have of ourselves, is this not? But why would God have such an assessment of the whole human race? For the answer to that question, we need to be aware that God is Creator of all that exists, so that when God created the first man, Adam, at the beginning of time, God created him in innocence, meaning that Adam as first created by God neither knew good nor evil, nor was there any sin anywhere in God's original sinless creation.

However, the day came when God tested Adam with a command, saying to him in the garden of Eden here on earth, which was the perfect environment which God had for him, what we now read at Genesis 2:16,17, "[16] The Lord God commanded the man, saying, "From any tree of the garden you may eat freely; [17] but from the tree of the knowledge of good and evil you shall not eat, for in the day that you eat from it you will surely die." How important to see here that God gave Adam, who although a real person was also representative of the whole human race, the warning of the penalty of death for disobedience to His command.

Unfortunately, the day did come when Adam did partake of the forbidden tree and thereby did sin against God. The moment that happened, Adam not only became a sinner by practice, but also a sinner by nature. One thing my parents had to continually do while under their care was to restrain me from continually going the wrong way, for it seemed that of myself I could not do good, but kept going into sin. The reason this was happening is that from the age of accountability onwards, I had not only become a sinner by practice, but also a sinner by nature.

And here the age of accountability needs to be seen as being when as a young child in innocence - which moment is known only by God - one comes to learn the right from the wrong and chooses the wrong, thereby becoming personally accountable to God for one's own sin against Him, since all sin is first of all against Him. And that is why God can say at Romans 3:23 above that "all have sinned and fall short of the glory of God," because God knows that all human beings will go the way of Adam, our representative man, which is also why God can say what He does in regards to the whole of the human race at Romans 5:12, where we read, "Therefore, just as through one man (Adam) sin entered into the world, and death through sin, and so death spread to all men, because all sinned" (from the age of accountability onward). And so, we see that the whole human race is declared by God to not only be sinners by practice and by nature from the age of accountability onwards, but the whole of the human race is now subject to death! In other words, in God's sight the whole of the human race is under the judgment of the penalty of death, due to all being sinners by practice and by nature.

You will recall above, in the first verse we quoted from Romans 6:23, God did say there that "the wages of sin are death." And what God means by "death" here is not just loss of physical life, when the physical body we have dies, but also has spiritual death in mind, which is far worse! Spiritual death has its beginning when a separation takes place between a person and God at the moment one becomes a sinner at the age of accountability and ends after the final judgment of time, when God forever casts away from His Presence those who before physical death refused to believe in His Son, The Lord Jesus Christ, thereby personally forfeiting the forgiveness of their sins and eternal life with God. And now all such will pay the penalty for their own sins in hell, away from the Presence of God forever.

It is in the midst of such a hopeless situation in which the whole of the human race found itself in that God TOOK THE INITIATIVE and sent His own eternally existing Son into the world, as born of a virgin in the innocence of Adam – so as not to inherit the sinful nature passed on from generation after generation from Adam onwards through the conception of the female – so that He might be the acceptable sacrifice offered to God His Father at the cross, there bearing our sins in His body, and there dying the death due our sins! God's Son, Jesus Christ, was then buried and raised from the dead the third day, to ever be alive, for it is through Him, on the basis of what God has done for us through His Son, that God The Father forgives our sins and imparts us eternal life.

Now, by God's grace and His enablement, may you see your need of God's Son to be Your Savior from the penalty due sin, which is death, not only physical, but also spiritual. And by God's grace, may He lead you to believe in His Son, Jesus Christ, and in believing, to receive the forgiveness of your sins and eternal life with Him forever! And based on the truth just shared, the author would now like to ask you a few questions, with the answer being just between yourself and God:

When God says at Romans 3:23, "for all have sinned and fall short of the glory of God," does that include you?

When God says at Romans 5:8, "But God demonstrates His own love toward us, in that while we were yet sinners, Christ died for us," were you included in Christ's death on behalf of sinners?

And when God further says at 1 Peter 3:18 in part, "For Christ also died for sins once for all, the just for the unjust, so that He might bring us to God, having been put to death in the flesh, but made alive in the spirit," were you part of the unjust for whom Christ died?

When God says at Romans 6:23, "For the wages of sin is death, but the free gift of God is eternal life in Christ Jesus our Lord," do you want that eternal life as a free gift from God?

When God says at John 3:16, "For God so loved the world, that He gave His only begotten Son, that whoever believes in Him shall not perish, but have eternal life," do you now believe that Jesus Christ is indeed God's Son in human flesh, Who came from Heaven to this earth to die in your place, so as to save you from ever experiencing the judgment of God leading to an eternal separation from God in hell?

And when God then further says to you at Isaiah 55:6, "Seek the Lord while He may be found; call upon Him while He is near," for His further promise to you here is as we read at Romans 10:9-11,13, "[9] that if you confess with your mouth Jesus as Lord, and believe in your heart that God raised Him from the dead, you will be saved (that is, you will now enter into a personal relationship with God by faith); [10] for with the heart a person believes, resulting in righteousness (that is, in now receiving God's own righteous and eternal life to live by), and with the mouth he confesses, resulting in salvation (that is, in now receiving as a free gift the forgiveness of sins and eternal life with God). [11] For the Scripture says, "Whoever believes in Him will not be disappointed..." [13] for "Whoever will call on the name of the Lord will be saved." Will you now call upon God from your heart in your own words being mindful of your answer to each question that have just been asked?

The author's prayer for you at this point, as you now call upon God by His grace, is what we read at Romans 15:13, "Now may the God of hope fill you with all joy and peace in believing, so that you will abound in hope by the power of the Holy Spirit."

/ The next book

As this book is being published, God has given His servant the go-ahead to write another book, titled "Why God created a woman!" In case it is not the next book, the reader may want to check with the author's website to see what book has been published:

http://www.pilgrimpathwaypublications.com

If you have found this book profitable, or any other of the author's books, please feel free to let family, friends, and co-workers know about this book and the other books. The author is not on any social media sites, so he relies on God and readers to spread the word. May God bless you for doing so!

www.ingramcontent.com/pod-product-compliance
Lightning Source LLC
Chambersburg PA
CBHW051216160726
47994CB00002B/628